ATTITUDE
IS A CHOICE
SO PICK A GOOD ONE

BOB PHILLIPS

HARVEST HOUSE PUBLISHERS
EUGENE, OREGON

Cover designer Studio Gearbox

Cover Photo © Stone background, Rawpixel.com / Shutterstock

Interior designer Rockwell Davis

"The Influence of Gratitude": Every attempt was made to find ownership of this so that we could provide attribution. If attribution is provided, it will be included in the next reprint of this book.

Attitude Is a Choice—So Pick a Good One
Copyright © 2023 by Bob Phillips
Published by Harvest House Publishers
Eugene, Oregon 97408
www.harvesthousepublishers.com

ISBN 978-0-7369-8685-4 (pbk.)
ISBN 978-0-7369-8686-1 (eBook)

Library of Congress Control Number: 2022945917

Printed in the United States of America

23 24 25 26 27 28 29 30 31 / BP / 10 9 8 7 6 5 4 3 2 1

Dedication to Betty Fletcher

I've been asked, "How do you know if you've written a bad book?" That's an easy question to answer. You know you've written a really bad book when even the editor won't read it. I'm grateful that you were kind enough to read my books.

Betty, I'm personally going to miss working with you. I have appreciated your insight, flexibility, and honesty. You have always been open to discuss new ideas, my crazy concepts, and my complicated layout designs.

The first person to really read your manuscript with a desire to make you a better communicator is the editor. Betty, you have been that person for me. You have added color and creativity. You have mastered the skill of the delete button by taking out everything that was not necessary or clear for the reader. You have helped me become a better writer. I want to thank you for that.

As you leave Harvest House with great memories, I pray the Lord will give you a new sense of adventure in what lies ahead for you. May the Lord bless you richly and use you greatly.

Table of Contents

HOW TO USE THIS BOOK

How would you rate the quality of your attitude at this time? Would you say it's great? Would you say it's poor? Or would you say your attitude could use some realignment, adjustment, and improvement? Regardless of your answer, this book is for you.

Basically, an attitude is nothing more than a personal thought process...and we choose what we think about.

> Choose a thought and reap an action.
> Choose an action and reap a habit.
> Choose a habit and reap a character.
> Choose a character and reap a destiny.

It has been said that no one else can make your choices for you. Your choices are yours alone. They're as much a part of you as every breath you take. The quality and success of your life is determined by your choices. Andy Stanley expresses the same thought when he says, "You write the story of your life...one decision at a time."[1] We take charge of our life when we take charge of our choices. Take addictions, for example. Addictions like drugs, alcohol, overeating, procrastination, lying, and more can be directly tied to decisions.

When choices become habits, they are more difficult to change. Without question, breaking negative habits and establishing positive habits requires work. Do you have negative attitudes you would like to change? Positive attitudes you would like to reinforce? Then this book can help.

Honestly, there's no middle ground. Either you're working on your positive attitudes or you're not working on them. To quote Yoda, "Do. Or do not. There is no try."

Would you like to have an engaged life, a pleasant life, a meaningful life, and a happier and healthier life? If so, change starts with your attitude. Change can happen when you realize it all begins with your choices.

You can choose to read this book by starting at the beginning and reading straight through to the end. Or you can pick and choose the chapters that draw your interest from the table of contents. Each of the various chapters was written as a stand-alone article.

- I would encourage you to read each chapter rapidly to get an overview. Then go back and read it more thoroughly…digesting the concepts.

- Stop frequently and ponder a thought or a quote that might apply to you.

- Have a pen, pencil, or colored marker available. Then underline or highlight important thoughts that stand out to you.

- Keep the book on your desk or nightstand. In this way, it will be there to help you review and be a resource reminder.

- We all learn best by becoming personally involved. Try to follow through with some of the "Attitude Exercises" suggested in the book.

- Keep a diary or journal of your successes in changing your attitude.

- Keep in mind that your goal is not to gain information. Your goal is to make choices that will help you establish positive habits, behaviors, and attitudes.

- You might want to begin by taking the "Attitude Evaluation Scale."

- I hope you will enjoy the journey.

Attitude

Positive   Negative

Attitude Is a Choice…So Pick a Good One.

ATTITUDE EVALUATION SCALE

*Circumstances do not make you what you
are. They reveal what you are.*

JOHN C. MAXWELL

	High (Positive)	Low (Negative)

1. I would rate my *present* attitude as a 10 9 8 7 6 5 4 3 2 1

2. My *kindness* and *concern* for others
   rates as a...10 9 8 7 6 5 4 3 2 1

3. My attitude while *driving* demands
   a rating of 10 9 8 7 6 5 4 3 2 1

4. My close *friends* would rate my
   attitude as a..10 9 8 7 6 5 4 3 2 1

5. My ability to make *decisions* deserves
   a rating of 10 9 8 7 6 5 4 3 2 1

6. My *enthusiasm* toward life and my *future*
   rates as a...10 9 8 7 6 5 4 3 2 1

7. My attitude toward *facing change* would
   register a 10 9 8 7 6 5 4 3 2 1

8. My ability to *set goals* and work toward them
   earns a...10 9 8 7 6 5 4 3 2 1

9. My *family* would say that my attitude rating
   should be 10 9 8 7 6 5 4 3 2 1

10. My ability to deal with *conflict* would
    rate a score of 10 9 8 7 6 5 4 3 2 1

11. My exercise of *patience* and *tolerance*
    deserves a rating of...10 9 8 7 6 5 4 3 2 1

12. My boss would say my attitude at *work*
    deserves a rating of...10 9 8 7 6 5 4 3 2 1

13. My attitude of *forgiving others* merits
    a score of..10 9 8 7 6 5 4 3 2 1

14. My ability to *not gripe, complain,* or *criticize*
    qualifies for a 10 9 8 7 6 5 4 3 2 1

15. My *happiness* level and *sense of humor* deserves
    a rating of 10 9 8 7 6 5 4 3 2 1

16. My display of *gratitude* on a consistent basis
    deserves a...10 9 8 7 6 5 4 3 2 1

17. My ability to be *self-controlled* and
    self-disciplined merits a 10 9 8 7 6 5 4 3 2 1

18. The score others might give me as a person
    who *smiles a lot* would be a.................................10 9 8 7 6 5 4 3 2 1

19. My tendency toward a *positive spirit* and
    positive comments deserves a 10 9 8 7 6 5 4 3 2 1

20. My tendency toward a *negative spirit* and
    negative comments deserves a 10 9 8 7 6 5 4 3 2 1

21. My effort to not let the *little things* get the best
    of me deserves a...10 9 8 7 6 5 4 3 2 1

22. My freedom from *anger, bitterness,* and
    resentment deserves a rating of..........................10 9 8 7 6 5 4 3 2 1

23. My freedom from *fear, anxiety,* and *worry*
    would register a score of...................................10 9 8 7 6 5 4 3 2 1

24. My freedom from *shyness* and *being*
    uncomfortable in groups deserves a...................10 9 8 7 6 5 4 3 2 1

25. My freedom from feelings of *inferiority* and a
    poor self-image registers as a 10 9 8 7 6 5 4 3 2 1

26. My freedom from present feelings of *hurt,*
    sadness, or *depression* gives me a score of............10 9 8 7 6 5 4 3 2 1

27. The way I respond to *food servers* and
    store clerks deserves a rating of 10 9 8 7 6 5 4 3 2 1

28. Those individuals *who work with me*
    might give me an attitude rating of..................10 9 8 7 6 5 4 3 2 1

29. My ability to express *appreciation* and
    show encouragement to others earns a................10 9 8 7 6 5 4 3 2 1

30. If I was suddenly ushered into the *presence of*
    God, He might give me an attitude rating of 10 9 8 7 6 5 4 3 2 1

                              TOTAL_____

A score of 226 or higher indicates you're *making positive attitude choices.*

A score between 151 and 225 indicates that *minor adjustments* may be needed.

A score between 76 and 150 indicates *a major attitude adjustment* is needed.

A score below 75 indicates that a *complete attitude overhaul* may be required.

You cannot control what happens to you, but you can control your attitude toward what happens to you, and in that, you will be mastering change rather than allowing it to master you.

BRIAN TRACY

Attitude Is a Choice...So Pick a Good One.

2

ATTITUDE DEFINITION

*If you change the way you look at things,
the things you look at change.*

WAYNE DYER

WEBSTER'S UNABRIDGED DICTIONARY: *Attitude is a manner of acting, feeling, or thinking that shows one's disposition or opinion.*

OXFORD DICTIONARY: *Attitude is a settled way of thinking or feeling about something.*

VARIOUS VIEWS:

*Attitudes are nothing more than habits of
thoughts, and habits can be acquired. An action
repeated becomes an attitude realized.*

PAUL MYER

*Your attitude is the outward display of
what you are thinking inside.*

TRACIE MILES

*Very little is needed to make a happy life. It is all within
yourself—in your way of thinking and attitude.*

FRED CORBETT

*Attitude is nothing more (and nothing less) than the sum
total of all the small, daily choices we make or fail to make.*

SHAD HELMSTETTER

*Attitude is the librarian of our past, the speaker
of our present, and the prophet of our future.*

KEVIN PLANK

Ability is what you're capable of doing. Motivation determines what you do. Attitude determines how well you do it.

LOU HOLTZ

Our attitude is our personal boomerang to the world—whatever we throw out will come back to us.

TIM WRIGHT

Attitude improvement is much like bathing: It is something we recommend you do every day!

ZIG ZIGLAR

The greatest day in your life and mine is when we take total responsibility for our attitudes. That's the day we truly grow up.

JOHN C. MAXWELL

Your attitude should be the kind that was shown us by Jesus Christ, who, though he was God, did not demand and cling to his rights as God, but laid aside his mighty power and glory, taking the disguise of a slave and becoming like men. And he humbled himself ever further, going so far as actually to die a criminal's death on a cross.

PHILIPPIANS 2:5-8

PHILLIPS DEFINITION: *Attitude is a habit pattern arising from a complex mixture of positive or negative thinking, which produces helpful or hurtful emotions, and behavior.*

Jim Rohn suggests that your thoughts or philosophy about life lay a foundation for your attitude. Your attitude then drives your words, actions, or behavior. The results of your actions end up producing a lifestyle.

He goes on to say: "If you don't like your lifestyle, look at the results. If you don't like your results, look at your actions. If you don't like your actions, look at your attitude. If you don't like your attitude, look at your philosophy."

What is your philosophy? How do you view the world?

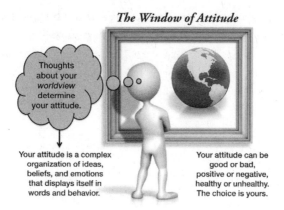

The Window of Attitude

Thoughts about your *worldview* determine your attitude.

Your attitude is a complex organization of ideas, beliefs, and emotions that displays itself in words and behavior.

Your attitude can be good or bad, positive or negative, healthy or unhealthy. The choice is yours.

A bad attitude is like a flat tire. You can't go anywhere till you change it.

When Charles Dickens wrote *A Tale of Two Cities,* he opened the story by saying,

> It was the best of times, it was the worst of times, it was the age of wisdom, it was the age of foolishness, it was the epoch of belief, it was the epoch of incredulity, it was the season of Light, it was the season of Darkness, it was the spring of hope, it was the winter of despair, we had everything before us, we had nothing before us, we were all going direct to Heaven, we were all going direct the other way—in short, the period was so far like the present period, that some of its noisiest authorities insisted on its being received, for good or for evil, in the superlative degree of comparison only.

He was suggesting that life is filled with good and bad, positives and negatives, hope and despair.

"So what?" you may ask.

You have a choice. The negatives and difficulties in life can overcome you, or you can choose to be an overcomer. You can choose to believe that all of creation just happened and that life has no purpose...you just have to make the best you can with your circumstances. Or you can choose to believe a Creator God has a plan and purpose for your life.

If there is no God, you're only accountable to yourself for what you think, believe, say, and do. Your attitude can be anything you want it to be. You are only responsible for yourself in all areas of life.

If, on the other hand, you believe in a Creator God, then you become responsible and accountable for what you think, believe, say, and do. Your attitude then becomes answerable to your Maker.

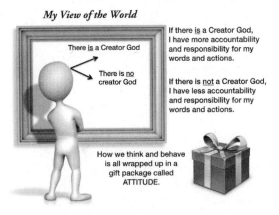

My View of the World

There is a Creator God

There is no creator God

If there is a Creator God, I have more accountability and responsibility for my words and actions.

If there is not a Creator God, I have less accountability and responsibility for my words and actions.

How we think and behave is all wrapped up in a gift package called ATTITUDE.

Dear God,

Please help me to become aware of the importance of my attitude…not only for my own emotional health and well-being, but also for the health and well-being of my family and friends. Help me to make peace with the difficult issues of life that I am facing. Help me discover Your purpose for my life. I know I will be happier if I learn to trust You. Teach me to be alert to those negative thoughts that bring about a negative spirit in me. Help me to relax my control on my life and become more dependent on You. I want to be accountable and responsible to You. I need Your help and guidance.

Amen.

Attitude Is a Choice…So Pick a Good One.

ATTITUDE AND COMPLEXITY

For all their expertise at figuring out how things work,
technical people are often painfully aware how much
of human behavior is a mystery. People do things for
unfathomable reasons. They are opaque even to themselves.

GARY WOLF

You just blew it again! Why can't you keep your stupid mouth shut?
Every time you get in a group and try to join the conversation, you
make a fool of yourself. You know you're not smart and cool like the others.
You'd be better off to just stay at home. You know you don't have any real
friends...and with the way you think and talk, you're never going to get
new friends!

It was another bad day for Ashley. Making friends had been difficult
for her since grade school. Now that she was in college, the situation had
gotten even worse. She had always been shy, and now she found herself
withdrawing more and more. She knew she wasn't fitting in, and her
loneliness was growing. She had even begun to think that life was not
worth living. She could tell her depression was intensifying.

You cannot keep birds from flying over your head,
but you can keep them from building a nest in your hair.

MARTIN LUTHER

The great reformer, Martin Luther, compared his thoughts to the birds that fly over your head. You don't control the birds…and you don't always have control of the thoughts that enter your mind. Your thoughts can be positive or negative. They can be good thoughts or bad thoughts. They can be based on facts, or they can be totally out of touch with reality. The truth is, you can't stop them from flying through your brain. But the reformer suggested that you *can* stop the birds from making a home out of your hair. You do have control—*and the decision-making power*—to retain certain thoughts or dismiss them from your thinking.

But dismissing certain thoughts is not always an easy task. It might even be very difficult and painful if we have been hurt emotionally. Negative thoughts create the foundation for poor or bad attitudes.

Where do negative thoughts come from? How are attitudes created? They come from the same place positive thoughts come from.

They begin in our families of origin. Your family may make some comment that hurts you or helps you. They may act in ways that don't match up to your expectations, or they may meet those expectations. You may have some experience that doesn't address your need for love and acceptance, or you may experience love and not rejection. When we

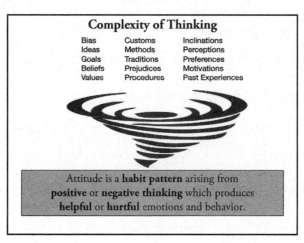

grow older, we add various experiences with relatives, friends, teachers, schoolmates, coworkers, bosses, civil authorities, and even strangers.

As we grow and learn, our thinking processes become more and more complex. From all this complexity, our attitudes are formed. Our attitudes then provide energy for either positive or negative words and deeds.

> *Watch your thoughts for they become words.*
> *Watch your words for they become actions.*
> *Watch your actions for they become habits.*
> *Watch your habits for they become your character.*
> *And watch your character for it becomes your destiny.*
> *What we think, we become.*
>
> **MARGARET THATCHER**

THOUGHTS are series of words that travel through the mind. They can be good or bad thoughts, right or wrong thoughts, or positive or negative thoughts.

- *You should apologize. You shouldn't have said what you just said!*

- *You did a good job on the last project. You can never do anything right!*

- *You're being very kind. You're acting like such an idiot!*

URGES are often referred to as desires or wants—impulses or drives—or temptations or turn-ons. They create a strong feeling or pressure to say something or do some type of activity.

- *Just try that drug and see if it will give you a sense of happiness, euphoria, or fulfillment!*

- *If she ever puts you down again, tell her where she can go in no uncertain terms—even if she is the boss!*

- *That piece of chocolate cake is what I need…now!*

SENSATIONS are physical reactions triggered in the body.

- My back itches.
- My head aches.
- My heart is pounding.
- I can't catch my breath.
- I'm thirsty.

- My hand is shaky.
- I feel my face getting red.
- I'm hot.
- Something in my eye is making it water.

EMOTIONS are a whirlwind mix of thoughts, urges, and sensations together. They are often expressed by single words, such as:

- Anger
- Depression
- Fear

- Grief
- Happiness
- Hate

- Joy
- Love
- Sadness

Choosing the proper attitude begins with identifying and understanding the four above factors and how they produce actions and behavior.

Okay, I get it. But how do I stop the birds from building a nest in my hair?

A good place to start is to give your negative thoughts a name. Luther called them "birds," but you could say, "The *buzzards* are flying today." Or you might say, "The *donkeys* are braying." Or, if you like other animals, you might say, "The *monkeys* are dancing."

You could choose to imagine yourself sitting down and watching a train approaching: "Here comes the *drain train*." If you prefer, you might envision yourself on a boat with a leak: "I think my *boat is sinking*." Have some fun by coming up with your own creative name for negative thoughts. I prefer to use a martial arts illustration of "Battling Big Bully." By giving negative thoughts a name like "Big Bully," you begin to rob them of the power to control your emotions, words, and actions.

The best way to deal with bullies is to face them and identify them for what they are. Bully thoughts are our own personal terrorists. Bully thoughts attempt to control us through fear of what others think or how we are being received, or they compel us to get angry and strike out at those who seem to be against us.

We would worry less about what others think of us
if we realized how seldom they do.

Big Bully terrorists like to speak with a lot of *shoulds*.

SHOULDS	TRUTH
• You should always be friendly.	*No one is always friendly.*
• You should never make mistakes.	*Everyone makes mistakes.*
• You should never be afraid.	*We should be afraid at times.*
• You should be perfect.	*Hello. No one is perfect.*
• You should be totally self-reliant.	*We all need help from others.*
• You should always work hard.	*Sometimes we need to rest.*
• You should never get angry.	*Sometimes it's right to be angry.*
• You should always be kind.	*That's a good ideal to shoot for.*
• You should never have bad thoughts.	*Who has never had bad thoughts?*
• You should never feel sad.	*When a loved one dies, sadness is normal.*

Big Bully terrorists thrive on cataclysmic overgeneralizations and absolute terms that whip you into a guilty frenzy—words like *all, every, none, everybody, never,* and *always.*

All you do is make an idiot of yourself.
Every time you do something, you fail.
None of the people who know you like you.
Everybody thinks you're a loser.

Never do I see you doing anything for others.
Always being late is what makes people dislike you.

Big Bully terrorists like to use all-encompassing disapproving descriptions like:

- Bum
- Clumsy
- Coward
- Cracked
- Crazy
- Dull

- Failure
- Flop
- Hopeless
- Inferior
- Lazy
- Loser

- Obnoxious
- Silly
- Slob
- Stupid
- Ugly
- Weak

Big Bully terrorists like to use the "dirty dozen" to convince you that you have no control. You can do nothing about your circumstances or the situation you're in, so you have an excuse to be a victim with no power to change.

1. It's not your fault.
2. There's no escape.
3. Your situation is sad and hopeless.
4. You're doing it again.
5. You can't break that habit.
6. You'll never get organized.
7. There's nothing you can do.
8. Your head is just above water.
9. You'll never get out of your depression.
10. You're going to feel this pain forever and ever.
11. You are at the end of your rope with nowhere to go.
12. You can look forward to doing this the rest of your life.

Big Bully terrorists know you have an extreme vulnerability to criticism, so they compare you to others and note how inferior you are to them. They like to set impossible standards that you cannot possibly fulfill and keep a diary of all your failures. They want to keep you timid, shy, and worthless. They relish seeing you wallow in the misery of guilt and regret.

In the human body, we have a mechanism called the immune system. Its job is to protect your body from any toxins, diseases, or viruses using cells designed to attack any foreign substances. Once in a while, though, the body will make a mistake and attack healthy cells. This self-destroying process is called an autoimmune disease.

When negative thoughts begin to make a nest in your mind, they give you an "emotional autoimmune disease." Our mind, in a sense, is attacking itself in a debilitating way. This unproductive process needs to end.

When you get an unwanted call on your cell phone, what do you do? First you acknowledge that the call has come in. You do this by typing the phone number into your contacts file. Then you scroll down a little and click on the button that says *Block this Caller*. Done!

Similarly, the first thing you do with negative thoughts is to acknowledge that they are attempting to make a nest in your thinking pattern. Next, try to identify the strategy of Big Bully terrorists when they fire their overgeneralizations and *shoulds* at you. Their terror tactic is to make you into a victim who has no power to change or escape.

The next step is to block these thoughts. You no longer want to deal with the negativity. You do this by saying aloud: "Stop! Enough! Knock it off!" The speaking out loud is a bit of a shock to your internal thinking process. Now alert, you better understand you don't have to be a victim of the Big Bully. The spoken words help you realize you have a choice: to keep on wallowing in negativity or to get out of the swamp and change your thinking to positive thoughts.

> *The greatest discovery of my generation is that human beings*
> *can alter their lives by altering their attitude of mind…*
> *If you change your mind, you can change your life.*
>
> **WILLIAM JAMES**

Finally, brothers and sisters, whatever is true, whatever
is noble, whatever is right, whatever is pure, whatever is
lovely, whatever is admirable—if anything is excellent or
praiseworthy—think about such things. Whatever you have
learned or received or heard from me, or seen in me—put
it into practice. And the God of peace will be with you.

PHILIPPIANS 4:8-9 NIV

─── Awareness Project ───

Over the next week, attempt to become aware of situations that trigger your thoughts, urges, sensations, and emotions. The more alert you are to the four triggers, the more you can *choose* to make *positive choices* about your attitude rather than *negative choices*.

A problem well stated is a problem half solved.

CHARLES KETTERING

Put a check mark next to the proper trigger you became alert to—and describe the choice you made as a response to that particular trigger.

Example: ☐ **Thought** ☑ **Urge** ☐ **Sensation** ☐ **Emotion**

Chosen Response:

During the morning break time, I heard the horn on the snack truck outside our building. My usual habit is to buy something. Today I chose not to purchase anything to see if I could control and change my expensive, unhealthy habit.

Example: ☑ **Thought** ☐ **Urge** ☐ **Sensation** ☐ **Emotion**

Chosen Response:

During staff meetings I'm usually silent and rarely share anything. Today I chose to contribute an idea. I felt an internal struggle but finally spoke up. To my surprise, my suggestion was well received by the group.

—— Now It's Your Turn ——

Sunday: ☐ Thought ☐ Urge ☐ Sensation ☐ Emotion
Chosen Response:

_____

_____

_____

Monday: ☐ Thought ☐ Urge ☐ Sensation ☐ Emotion
Chosen Response:

_____

_____

_____

Tuesday: ☐ Thought ☐ Urge ☐ Sensation ☐ Emotion
Chosen Response:

_____

_____

_____

Wednesday: ☐ Thought ☐ Urge ☐ Sensation ☐ Emotion
Chosen Response:

_____

_____

_____

Thursday: ☐ Thought ☐ Urge ☐ Sensation ☐ Emotion
Chosen Response:

_____

_____

_____

Friday: ☐ **Thought**   ☐ **Urge**   ☐ **Sensation**   ☐ **Emotion**
Chosen Response:

_____

_____

_____

Saturday: ☐ **Thought**   ☐ **Urge**   ☐ **Sensation**   ☐ **Emotion**
Chosen Response:

_____

_____

_____

What did you learn about making choices with regard to thoughts, urges, sensations, and emotions?

_____

_____

_____

_____

_____

_____

*Sometimes it's the smallest decisions
that change your life forever.*

KERI RUSSELL

*Life is a matter of choices, and every
choice you make, makes you.*

JOHN MAXWELL

Make good choices today so you don't have regrets tomorrow.

R.E. PHILLIPS

Dear God,

I need You to help me take control of the strange and unwanted thoughts that fly through my brain like birds. Help me ignore the urge to make cutting remarks, and the desire to get even with those who have hurt me. Make me aware of various physical sensations that indicate I'm under stress or dealing with difficult emotions. Help me not to become overwhelmed with unfair *shoulds* that place me under the control of unrealistic expectations. Give me the strength to toss out negative thoughts that attack my thinking like terrorists. Help me to put honest effort into the Awareness Project, and help me make changes in my attitude. Thank You for Your help.

Amen.

Attitude Is a Choice...So Pick a Good One.

ATTITUDE AND SELF-IMAGE

*The "self-image" is the key to human personality
and human behavior. Change the self-image and
you change the personality and the behavior.*

Maxwell Maltz

My first impression of Michael was one of sadness. As he entered my office, his shoulders drooped forward and his head faced downward. It seemed like he was carrying a heavy burden on his back. His eyes glanced at me and then back toward his feet. He shuffled forward and plopped himself into a chair like a sack of potatoes. He then let out a long, deep sigh.

"How are you doing today, Michael?" I said, trying to lighten his spirits.

"Not good. It's been a terrible week." He responded without looking at me.

Michael then proceeded to unload his anxieties. He talked about his inability to make and keep friends. He felt it was because of his poor communication skills. He admitted that he was very shy and found it difficult to share his feelings with others. He expressed how lonely he was. He thought he didn't have a positive personality. He didn't see others being drawn to him. He then began to talk about his looks. He thought his ears were too big. He said his nose was bent and his teeth were crooked. He then mentioned that he didn't have the skills and abilities others have, and that his boss didn't show any appreciation for him or his work. He felt like he didn't have any worth…to anyone.

Michael is not alone. Many people are not satisfied with their body image. They express deep concerns about the appearance of their:

Hair	Teeth	Stomach
Complexion	Mouth	Hips
Ears	Chin	Butt
Eyes	Neck	Legs
Nose	Shoulders	Feet
Lips	Arms	Toes

Often an overlap exists between the terms *self-esteem* and *self-image*. The biggest difference is that self-esteem focuses on *acceptance and worth*, whereas self-image involves *capabilities and self-fulfillment*.

Psychologist Abraham Maslow developed what he called a Hierarchy of Needs that outlines and ranks the needs people attempt to satisfy. When those needs are not met it tends to affect the individual's self-image. There are basic needs, psychological needs, and self-fulfillment needs. His diagram assists us in clarifying the difference between self-esteem needs and self-image or self-actualization needs.

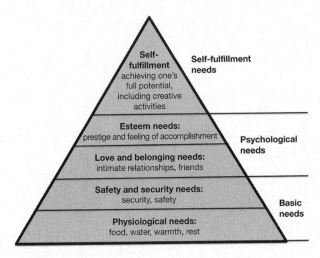

1. PHYSIOLOGICAL—food, water, sleep, warmth, breathing, and excretion.

2. SAFETY AND SECURITY—health and wellness, financial security, physical safety against accidents and injury, and job and property security.

3. LOVE AND BELONGING—family, friendships, romantic attachments, community groups, churches and religious organizations, and avoidance of loneliness.

4. ESTEEM—personal worth, acceptance, appreciation for and by others, respect, being valued, confidence, and personal contribution to the world.

5. SELF-FULFILLMENT—talents, capabilities, creativity, self-awareness, problem solving, acceptance of facts, fulfilling potential, less concerned with the opinion of others.

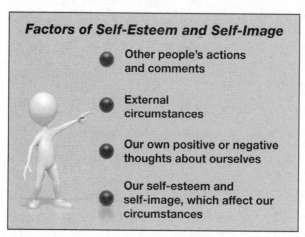

Factors of Self-Esteem and Self-Image

- Other people's actions and comments

- External circumstances

- Our own positive or negative thoughts about ourselves

- Our self-esteem and self-image, which affect our circumstances

Other People's Actions and Comments That Affect Us

- When you're not invited to a party, not asked to join a team, or ignored when you raise your hand to ask a question, you tend to feel unworthy, unloved, and lonely as a result. However, if you are invited to a party, join a team, or have your questions answered by others, you feel wanted and part of a group.

- When your parents say, "You're a loser. You never do anything right," or, "You're such a crybaby," their words crush your spirit. On the other hand, when they say they are proud of you and they trust you, it lifts your spirit. A kind word at the right time creates positive feelings.

*Surround yourself with positive people who believe
in your dreams, encourage your ideas, support your
ambitions, and bring out the best in you.*

ROY T. BENNETT

External Circumstances That Affect Self-Esteem and Self-Image

- If the company you work for has to lay people off and you can't find another job, your self-image could suffer. You could be thinking to yourself: *I'm not a good provider for my family.*

- If your son or daughter gets in trouble at school, you might want to be hard on yourself by thinking: *What did I do wrong in my parenting?*

*The happiness of your life depends upon
the quality of your thoughts.*

MARCUS AURELIUS

Our Own Thoughts—Positive or Negative—About Ourselves

- *I asked a stupid question in class and feel like an idiot.*
- *I'm getting so fat, and all of my clothes are frumpy.*
- *I'm so shy I'll never get married.*
- *I did all right on the test.*
- *I was able to help Carol deal with the difficult issue she was facing.*
- *I could tell my supervisor was very happy with my presentation to the group.*

*You only have control over three things in your
life—the thoughts you think, the images you
visualize, and the actions you take.*

JACK CANFIELD

Our Self-Esteem and Self-Image, Which Affect Our Circumstances

Embracing a positive attitude about your skills, abilities, and personal interaction with others could help you get a promotion at work. It might increase the possibility of meeting new people or even a future mate. Being positive attracts people to you. No one really wants to spend a lot of time with negative and pessimistic personalities.

> *Action is a great restorer and builder of confidence.*
> *Inaction is not only the result but the cause of fear.*
> *Perhaps the action you take will be successful; perhaps*
> *different action or adjustments will have to follow.*
> *But any action is better than no action at all.*
>
> NORMAN VINCENT PEALE

A low self-image can be a terrible burden to carry around. Maxwell Maltz suggests that "Low self-esteem is like driving through life with your hand brake on." Those with low self-image:

- experience low energy levels
- experience loss of motivation
- are easily discouraged
- are filled with self-doubt
- feel powerless to change
- are oversensitive and introspective
- have difficulty setting boundaries in relationships
- become people pleasers and struggle to say no
- feel worthless
- believe they have nothing to bring to the table

Listed below is a *Self-Esteem and Self-Image Inventory*. Take a few moments to review the positive and negative traits, then place a check mark next to the ones you think apply to you. When you are finished, count the total number of positive traits and the total number of negative traits.

Self-Esteem and Self-Image Inventory
Check the Words You Feel Best Describe You at This Time

POSITIVE TRAITS

- ❏ Active
- ❏ Adaptable
- ❏ Adventurous
- ❏ Agreeable
- ❏ Alert
- ❏ Ambitious
- ❏ Assertive
- ❏ Attentive
- ❏ Brave
- ❏ Calm
- ❏ Careful
- ❏ Caring
- ❏ Cheerful
- ❏ Compassionate
- ❏ Composed
- ❏ Confident
- ❏ Courageous
- ❏ Courteous
- ❏ Creative
- ❏ Curious
- ❏ Decisive
- ❏ Dependable
- ❏ Determined
- ❏ Diligent
- ❏ Disciplined

- ❏ Easygoing
- ❏ Efficient
- ❏ Energetic
- ❏ Enthusiastic
- ❏ Flexible
- ❏ Forgiving
- ❏ Friendly
- ❏ Funny
- ❏ Generous
- ❏ Gentle
- ❏ Gracious
- ❏ Happy
- ❏ Healthy
- ❏ Honest
- ❏ Hopeful
- ❏ Humorous
- ❏ Independent
- ❏ Intelligent
- ❏ Intuitive
- ❏ Joyful
- ❏ Kind
- ❏ Logical
- ❏ Loyal
- ❏ Methodical
- ❏ Optimistic
- ❏ Organized
- ❏ Patient

- ❏ Perfectionist
- ❏ Playful
- ❏ Practical
- ❏ Punctual
- ❏ Quiet
- ❏ Relaxed
- ❏ Reliable
- ❏ Resourceful
- ❏ Responsible
- ❏ Sensitive
- ❏ Sincere
- ❏ Sociable
- ❏ Strong
- ❏ Sympathetic
- ❏ Thoughtful
- ❏ Tolerant
- ❏ Trusting
- ❏ Wise
- ❏ Witty

NEGATIVE TRAITS

- ❏ Abrasive
- ❏ Aggressive
- ❏ Aimless
- ❏ Angry
- ❏ Antisocial

- ❑ Anxious
- ❑ Apathetic
- ❑ Arrogant
- ❑ Bitter
- ❑ Blunt
- ❑ Boring
- ❑ Bossy
- ❑ Caustic
- ❑ Complacent
- ❑ Conceited
- ❑ Cowardly
- ❑ Critical
- ❑ Cruel
- ❑ Cynical
- ❑ Deceitful
- ❑ Demanding
- ❑ Depressed
- ❑ Discouraged
- ❑ Disloyal
- ❑ Disobedient
- ❑ Egocentric
- ❑ Envious
- ❑ Flaky
- ❑ Forgetful
- ❑ Fussy
- ❑ Greedy
- ❑ Grumpy
- ❑ Gullible
- ❑ Harsh
- ❑ Hostile
- ❑ Impatient
- ❑ Impulsive
- ❑ Indecisive
- ❑ Inhibited
- ❑ Intolerant
- ❑ Irresponsible
- ❑ Jealous
- ❑ Judgmental
- ❑ Lazy
- ❑ Materialistic
- ❑ Messy
- ❑ Moody
- ❑ Naïve
- ❑ Neglectful
- ❑ Nervous
- ❑ Obnoxious
- ❑ Obsessive
- ❑ Pessimistic
- ❑ Prejudiced
- ❑ Quarrelsome
- ❑ Resentful
- ❑ Revengeful
- ❑ Rigid
- ❑ Rude
- ❑ Sarcastic
- ❑ Selfish
- ❑ Stubborn
- ❑ Sullen
- ❑ Tactless
- ❑ Ungrateful
- ❑ Unkind
- ❑ Vengeful
- ❑ Weak-willed
- ❑ Whiny
- ❑ Withdrawn
- ❑ Worried

How did you do? Did you check more positive traits, or did you check more negative traits?

When it comes to counseling yourself, the *first thing* that must take place is to identify what's going on in your life. Are you experiencing more positives or more negatives?

The *second thing* is to clarify how you are feeling about what is going on. Are you happy about the positive traits? Are you dissatisfied with the negative traits?

The *third thing*—the most important thing—is to ask yourself this question: Do you want to change what's going on in your life, or are you happy with it? Actually, there's no way to avoid a choice. You will either choose to change or choose to continue what you're already doing. But the truth is, both are decisions. You're only fooling yourself if you think ignoring a choice isn't making one. That's why this book is entitled *Attitude Is a Choice*.

There are two primary choices in life: to accept conditions as they exist, or accept the responsibility for changing them.

DENIS WAITLEY

What Does God Say About Your Self-Image?

God created man in His own image; in the image of God He created him; male and female He created them (Genesis 1:27 NKJV).

I will praise You, for I am fearfully and wonderfully made; Marvelous are Your works (Psalm 139:14 NKJV).

Do not look at his appearance or at his physical stature...For the LORD does not see as man sees; for man looks at the outward appearance, but the LORD looks at the heart (1 Samuel 16:7 NKJV).

For we are His workmanship, created in Christ Jesus for good works, which God prepared beforehand that we should walk in them (Ephesians 2:10 NKJV).

Put on the new self, which in the likeness of God has been created in righteousness and holiness of the truth (Ephesians 4:24 NASB).

And do not be conformed to this world, but be transformed by the renewing of your mind, that you may prove what the will of God is, that which is good and acceptable and perfect (Romans 12:2 NASB).

Have this attitude in yourselves which was also in Christ Jesus (Philippians 2:5 NASB).

Whatever you do in word or deed, do everything in the name of the Lord Jesus, giving thanks through Him to God the Father (Colossians 3:17 NASB).

It should be the hidden person of the heart, with the imperishable quality of a gentle and quiet spirit, which is precious in the sight of God (1 Peter 3:4 NASB).

Dear God,

I'm beginning to gain insight that self-esteem is more about acceptance and worth, while self-image involves capabilities and fulfillment. Sometimes I feel like I'm struggling with both of them. Help me to separate the issues so I can be more effective in dealing with them. Help me not to be overcome and destroyed by other people's comments and actions. Give me wisdom to face difficult circumstances when they come. Give me the courage and strength to control my negative thoughts. Help me to focus on the positive things in my life. Help me to understand how to change my circumstances by turning negative thinking into optimistic thinking. Help me to understand that it's more important how You view me than how other people view me. I want to change. Please help me to choose a positive attitude in all areas of my life.

Amen.

Attitude Is a Choice...So Pick a Good One.

5

ATTITUDE AND DEPRESSION

Mental pain is less dramatic than physical pain, but it is more common and also more hard to bear. The frequent attempt to conceal mental pain increases the burden: it is easier to say "My tooth is aching" than to say "My heart is broken."

C.S. LEWIS

Sadness was written all over Megan's face when she walked into my office. She sighed deeply as she slumped down in a chair. She looked like she was drained of energy.

I smiled and said, "Good to see you, Megan. How are things going for you?" I had a pretty good idea by her body language that she was not having a good day.

"Well…" She hesitated for a moment. "Things are not going well. I'm very depressed. My sleep pattern is out of whack, my stomach is upset, and I've been having headaches. I have a hard time concentrating and making decisions, and I feel overwhelmed. I feel like crawling into a hole to die."

"How long have you been feeling this way? How long have you been depressed?"

She stopped for a moment, and I could see her eyes roll up and a little to the right as if she was contemplating her answer.

"In all honesty, I think I've been depressed for about two years."

As a counselor, I'm fully aware that depression is a reaction to some event or circumstance. Nine times out of ten it revolves around, or is caused by, some type of disappointment, loss, or damaged relationship.

"What happened to you two years ago?" I asked. "Did someone say something that hurt your feelings? Was your reputation damaged or put into question? Did someone do something hurtful to you? Did you have expectations that were unmet? Were your actions misunderstood? Or were you involved in a situation that turned out to be totally unfair against you?"

Most depression arises or is caused by some type of hurt. When the hurt is not resolved, anger raises its ugly head. Then anger creates the desire to retaliate and to get some type of revenge for any unfairness.

- The National Institute of Mental Health suggests that 17.3 million American adults are dealing with depression. They also indicate that depression is more prevalent in women, who are almost twice as likely to encounter depression than men.

- The World Health Organization indicates that depression is a worldwide issue that affects 264 million people.

The Substance Abuse and Mental Health Services Administration has broken down the four major categories of depression.

1. *Situational*—due to the loss of a job, loss of a relationship, loss of a home through fire or flood, or the death of a loved one.

2. *Physical*—due to sleep loss, sickness, improper diet, drugs, alcohol, or chemical imbalances within the body.

3. *Psychological*—due to negative self-image, self-pity, faulty reasoning, and unresolved conflict with people.

4. *Spiritual*—due to feelings of emptiness, meaninglessness, guilt, and alienation from God.

Have you been experiencing depression? If so, I encourage you to attempt to determine when it started. Next, pause and take a moment and go to your "memory bank." Was your depression triggered by some disappointment, hurt, anger, loss, loneliness, or guilt? Novelist Jeffrey

Eugenides once wrote: "Depression is like a bruise that never goes away. A bruise in your mind. You just got to be careful not to touch it where it hurts. It's always there, though."

> *In this sad world of ours sorrow comes to all and it often comes with bitter agony. Perfect relief is not possible except with time. You cannot now believe that you will ever feel better. But this is not true. You are sure to be happy again. Knowing this, truly believing it will make you less miserable now. I have had enough experience to make this statement.*
>
> **Abraham Lincoln**

The first step to getting out of the pit of despair—*depression*—is to realize that you're in the pit. The second step is to ask yourself if you want to get out. "That's a stupid question," you say. Not really. Some people like the pit. Some people enjoy the pain. Some people get attention when they're in the pit. They would rather have the attention or a depressive attitude than relief from their misery. You can choose to fight depression with clear thinking, or you can choose to continue wallowing in your misery. You see, this entire book is about choice.

> *People have a hard time letting go of their suffering. Out of a fear of the unknown, they prefer suffering that is familiar.*
>
> **Thích Nhat Hanh**

There are two major models for dealing with depression and mental health. One is the *medical model* and the other is the *counseling model*. Some in the health field attempt to combine the two. The *medical model* relies on the concept that chemical imbalance in the body brings about depression and other mental health issues. Therefore, drugs are used to address the imbalance, which brings about a dependence on drugs for relief. Pharmaceutical companies love this model and promote it frequently on television and in various ads.

The Battle for Mental Health

Medical Model	Counseling Model
Mental Illness or Mental Disease	Mental Illness or Mental Disease

Cause	Cause
Chemical Imbalance in the Body	Buildup of Stresses from Many Sources

Result	Result
Mental and Emotional Disruption Physical Symptoms Acting-Out Behaviors	Mental & Emotional Disruption Physical Symptoms Acting-Out Behaviors

Course of Action	Course of Action
Tendency to Seek Outside Blame for Emotions and Behavior and Prescribe Drugs to Deal with the Problem	Tendency to Take Ownership for Emotions and Behavior and to Become Healthy Apart from Taking Drugs

Discouragement   Hope

The big question is: Did the chemical imbalance in the body cause the depression, or did mental depression bring about chemical change in the individual? Does a nervous stomach cause worry and anxiety, or do worry and anxiety cause a nervous stomach? I think you already know the answer.

Everyone has a choice in the mental health plan they want to follow. I personally believe the *counseling model* is the most effective when combined with spiritual counsel.

Although I have studied in the field of psychology and counseling for over 50 years, I have a very difficult time pointing to truly successful and long-lasting methods of counseling apart from the use of the Bible.

In my opinion, because Scripture offers great counsel, a close Christian friend who uses God's Word can be effective in helping you face the difficulties of life—*and cheaper*. Your minister could also be more beneficial to you than someone trained solely as a therapist.

Let's zero in a little on your depression. Try to focus on the hurt, loss, or disappointment you're feeling. Carl Jung suggested: "The foundation of all mental illness is the unwillingness to experience legitimate suffering." M. Scott Peck also comments about hurt when he says, "This tendency to avoid problems and the emotional suffering inherent in them is the primary basis of all human mental illness." He goes on to say, "Once we truly know that life is difficult—once we truly understand and accept it—then life is no longer difficult. Because once it is accepted, the fact that life is difficult no longer matters."

Who hasn't been hurt by something someone has said or done? We're all in the same boat. We've all been hurt. We're all suffering to one degree or another. I know no one who has not been hurt. Now that we've got that settled, what are you going to do about it? The way out of the pit is to admit you're hurt, face your hurt, let go of the hurt, and forgive the person who has hurt you.

Everything inside you might cry out: "That's not fair!"

You're right. It's not fair. But is holding onto your hurt and anger working for you? Has your constant mulling over the offense helped you move on with life?

Maybe it's time to choose a positive attitude and approach. Nobody said life would be easy. It may be totally impossible to put the egg back into a broken shell. Accept that fact, then look away from your depression and look toward helping and encouraging others. It's time to start making omelets out of broken eggs.

> *Every time there are losses there are choices to be made. You choose to live your losses as passages to anger, blame, hatred, depression, and resentment, or you choose to let these losses be passages to something new, something wider, and deeper.*
>
> HENRI NOUWEN

The best cure for depression is to ask God for help and then take action. You see, depression slows you down. It makes you want to withdraw. It robs you of energy. It causes you to focus your thinking on your own problems and hurts.

R.C. Sproul makes the following suggestion,

> When you feel depressed, it helps to actively change your environment. Go and do something different. Martin Luther conquered his depression by going outside to work in his garden. Surprisingly enough, one of the best ways to handle depression is to go to work immediately on the task you least enjoy.

Or, better yet, try to think of someone who could use your help today—someone in need of emotional encouragement, psychological assistance, financial uplifting, or spiritual support. Then get in your car and drive to their home. That way, you are getting out of yourself in order to meet *his or her* need. Pass on to them the same help and comfort that Christ has provided for you.

> *Blessed be the God and Father of our Lord Jesus Christ,*
> *the Father of mercies and God of all* comfort, *who* comforts
> *us in all our tribulation, that we may be able to* comfort *those*
> *who are in any trouble, with the* comfort *with which we*
> *ourselves are* comforted *by God. For as the sufferings of*
> *Christ abound in us, so our consolation*
> *also abounds through Christ.*
>
> 2 CORINTHIANS 1:3-5 NKJV, EMPHASIS ADDED

> *Experiencing a great sorrow is like entering a cave. We*
> *are overwhelmed by the darkness, the loneliness, the*
> *homesickness… We feel that there is no escape from the*
> *prison house of pain. But God in His loving-kindness*
> *has set on the invisible wall the Lamp of Faith—*
> *whose beams shall guide us back to the sunlit world*
> *where work and friends and service await us.*
>
> HELEN KELLER

Dear God,

There are days that I would just like to escape from it all. I feel like pulling the covers over my head so everything will disappear. I feel like I am sinking in quicksand and there is no way out. I guess I didn't realize how hurt I was. Not only am I hurt, but also I'm angry. Sometimes I just don't think it's fair the way things turn out. It shouldn't be this way. And yet it is this way.

God, I'm having a hard time accepting the facts. I struggle with wanting revenge. I want repayment, but I know that no price can erase the pain. I'm really tired of hurting. I'm tired of holding grudges. Please help me make peace with my pain. Help me to bear the burden of unfairness. When I realize how much pain, hurt, and disappointment You faced from others and from me—and how unfair it was—yet You chose to endure the suffering for me and forgive me, I see how I need to learn to do the same thing. Please help me to change my attitude and focus. I can't do it without You. Help me to get out of myself and become someone who can help others who are hurting and needing Your encouragement.

Amen.

Listen to my prayer, O God,
do not ignore my plea;
hear me and answer me.
My thoughts trouble me and I am distraught
because of what my enemy is saying,
because of the threats of the wicked;
for they bring down suffering on me
and assail me in their anger.
My heart is in anguish within me;
the terrors of death have fallen on me.
Fear and trembling have beset me;
horror has overwhelmed me.
I said, "Oh, that I had the wings of a dove!
I would fly away and be at rest.

I would flee far away
and stay in the desert;
I would hurry to my place of shelter,
far from the tempest and storm"…
As for me, I call to God,
and the LORD saves me. Evening, morning and noon
I cry out in distress,
and he hears my voice.
He rescues me unharmed
from the battle waged against me,
even though many oppose me…
My companion attacks his friends;
he violates his covenant.
His talk is smooth as butter,
yet war is in his heart;
his words are more soothing than oil,
yet they are drawn swords.
Cast your cares on the LORD
and he will sustain you;
he will never let
the righteous be shaken…
But as for me, I trust in you.

PSALM 55:1-8, 16-18, 20-22, 23 NIV

Often the waves of hurt strike the shoreline of memory.
But with time and God's help you can surf even large waves.

Attitude Is a Choice…So Pick a Good One.

6

ATTITUDE AND ANGER: PART ONE

*Anger is just anger. It isn't good. It isn't bad. It just is. What you
do with it is what matters. It's like anything else. You can use
it to build or to destroy. You just have to make the choice.*

JIM BUTCHER

Have you ever been in a fight? I don't mean a verbal argument; I mean a physical fight with fists flying and punches being thrown. It's not that fun. On one particular day, I could tell I was just seconds away from being hit.

At the summer camp I directed, I was walking across the grounds when I noticed a boy around 12 years of age looking around our fire truck. He picked up three fire-hose nozzles and walked toward the woods with them, so I followed and watched him toss them into the forest. He did not see me retrieve the nozzles. Then I followed him to his cabin.

With the nozzles in my hands, I introduced myself to his mother and related the behavior of her son. The boy's father saw me talking with the mother and came over to where we were standing. I shared with both of them what their son had done and the danger he might have caused by stealing the nozzles.

The father immediately became angry. He whipped off his belt and began to spank his son right in front of me. He then turned to me and said, "Get the hell out of here!" He stormed off, leaving me standing with his wife.

I said, "I am sorry for all this trouble, but I thought you would want to know about your son's behavior." To which the wife replied, "You had better leave. Don is really mad. Here he comes again. You should go."

As I turned to leave, I was confronted by the physical presence of

Don. I could tell he wanted to hit me. His face was red, his neck muscles were tight, and his fists were tightly clenched. Being trained in the martial arts, I knew a blow was about to erupt in my direction.

"Go ahead and hit me if you like," I said. "I have dealt as fairly and honestly with you as I know how." My words startled Don, making him pause for a moment. I continued to speak to him in a firm tone. My verbal comments prevented physical violence. Though Don was still angry and some issues were unresolved, we parted company and avoided a fistfight.

Anger is a universal emotion. Sometimes we are the ones who are angry; sometimes we are the recipients of other people's anger. Anger is a God-given emotion just like fear. Anger and fear are our friends if our anger is toward injustice or our fear protects us from harm. However, anger and fear can become our enemies if we turn them toward hurting others or running from issues that need to be resolved. The negative aspects of anger are influenced by:

- our clouded, old, and warped sin nature—which is basic selfishness

- our temperament and body chemistry. This could include our personality style (analytical, amiable, or expressive), along with things like low blood sugar and chemical imbalance

- our personal desires, demands, and expectations regarding our perceived needs

- the positive and negative modeling from our family of origin—parents and relatives who were examples

- positive and negative personal experiences and interpersonal relationships—watching others around us and interacting with them

- uncontrolled outside forces such as accidents, illness, natural disaster, and loss

Anger can express itself actively or passively. Active forms include criticism, sarcasm, and ridicule. Some people seem to get pleasure from putting others down. They say things like: "Is that your head—or did your body blow a bubble?" Or: "I don't recall your face, but your breath is familiar."

Psychologists tell us there are three reasons why we criticize others. First, we criticize the very things we are guilty of doing ourselves. Second, we criticize because we are unhappy about something, and we want others to join us in our unhappiness (the "misery loves company" syndrome).

Third, we criticize in order to elevate ourselves by lowering the character of others. Will Durant said, "To speak ill of others is a dishonest way of praising ourselves."

> *There is not the least thing can be said or done, but people will talk and find fault.*
> **MIGUEL DE CERVANTES**

Active anger can become more severe through gossip, humiliation, and slander. These forms seek to destroy the reputations of others. Anger is also revealed through physical acts of bullying, beating, and even murder. Suicide is also an extreme act of murder; the individual becomes angry enough to murder themselves.

The more common forms of anger take on passive expressions, such as silence. Nothing is quite so powerful and hurtful as shutting off communication with others. The Amish practice shunning to control the behavior of others. Silence will destroy a relationship quicker than any other method.

Many people who are upset don't like to admit they are angry. To describe their emotions, they use words such as *annoyed*, *irritated*, *frustrated*, and *exasperated*. I used to have a friend who would pound the table with his fist and yell, "I'm not mad! I'm not mad! I'm not mad!" Even though he said he was not mad, no one around agreed with him. His actions and body language told a different story. Deep-seated anger involves the concepts of disgust, repulsion, resentment, bitterness, and hatred. It's possible to smile and act cordial and still be filled with malice. Both men and women can express frustration and anger toward inanimate objects, disruptive situations, or toward people.

When you see a married couple coming down the street, the
one who is two or three steps ahead is the one that's mad.

HELEN ROWLAND

Anger is also a feature of depression. It's possible to be angry without being depressed, but it is not possible to be depressed without being angry. A classic sign of depression is a change in sleep patterns. The person has little or restless sleep or sleeps in overabundance.

What is your sleep pattern like? Have you been encountering depression? Are you aware of anger directed at some individual or a circumstance that's difficult? Has some hurt or loss come into your life? Often anger is the key that leads us to discover the hurt or loss that has not been dealt with or resolved.

Are you an angry person? Do you display an attitude of anger in an active way or a passive way? Or have you become an expert in displaying your anger in both active and passive forms?

Learning to deal with anger takes two basic tracks. The first is dealing with anger *before* becoming angry. The second is dealing with anger *after* becoming angry. Dealing with anger before you become angry is preventative maintenance; it's learning how to identify and rein in anger before it takes control. What follows are warning signs that indicate you may be dealing with some anger in your life. Place a check mark next to any of the physical indicators you are experiencing.

—— Physical Signs of Anger ——

- ❑ Accident proneness
- ❑ Asthma or hay fever
- ❑ Bladder problems
- ❑ Chest pains
- ❑ Constipation
- ❑ Diarrhea
- ❑ Heart problems
- ❑ Low back pain
- ❑ Migraine headaches
- ❑ Nausea and vomiting
- ❑ Neck pain
- ❑ Overeating

- ❑ Runny nose
- ❑ Skin rashes (hives, eczema)
- ❑ Starvation
- ❑ Stuttering
- ❑ Tension headaches

- ❑ Throat problems
- ❑ Twitches
- ❑ Ulcers
- ❑ Upset stomach

*Anger is nothing more than an outward
expression of hurt, fear, and frustration.*

R.E. PHILLIPS

Factors that Influence Anger

Place a check mark next to any factors that may be influencing anger in your life.

- ❑ Boredom
- ❑ Criticism
- ❑ Damaged love affair
- ❑ Drugs or alcohol
- ❑ Envy
- ❑ Expectations for others
- ❑ Family environment
- ❑ Fear of failure
- ❑ Feelings of helplessness
- ❑ Feelings of rejection
- ❑ Feelings of uselessness
- ❑ Frustration
- ❑ General stress
- ❑ Humiliation or embarrassment
- ❑ Ill health
- ❑ Injustice
- ❑ Insecurity

- ❑ Jealousy
- ❑ Lack of privacy
- ❑ Loss of goals
- ❑ Loss of a job
- ❑ Loss of a loved one through divorce or death
- ❑ Loss of respect
- ❑ Loss of sleep
- ❑ Mood swings
- ❑ Need for space
- ❑ Past experiences
- ❑ Physical injury or handicap
- ❑ Religious background
- ❑ Revenge
- ❑ Selfishness
- ❑ Social pressure
- ❑ Temperament
- ❑ Weather

Anger has the power to control your thinking process unless you keep it in check. If you're angry with someone or something, it can become an obsession. Anger can keep you up at night. It can ruin your health and destroy your relationships. Anger can cost you your job. Anger can become an attitude or a way of life for some people.

Do you get angry in certain locations? Do you get angry with certain individuals? Do specific situations trigger your anger? Take a moment to measure your anger with the following *Anger Inventory*. Rate your anger from 0 to 4 for each relationship or circumstance. This is a very general chart, so mark how you *usually* respond in tense situations. At the end of the inventory, total your score to get some idea of your involvement with anger and how it affects your attitude. Be sure to answer honestly.

—— Anger Inventory ——

0—I would feel very little or no annoyance.
1—I would feel a little irritated.
2—I would feel moderately upset.
3—I would feel quite angry.
4—I would feel very angry.

Circle the number that best describes the degree of anger you may be feeling.

1. Anger with my parents...0 1 2 3 4

2. Anger with my brothers 0 1 2 3 4

3. Anger with my sisters 0 1 2 3 4

4. Anger with my children 0 1 2 3 4

5. Anger with my spouse or significant other...................0 1 2 3 4

6. Anger with my in-laws 0 1 2 3 4

7. Anger with my current friends 0 1 2 3 4

8. Anger with my former friends......................................0 1 2 3 4

9. Anger with my neighbors...0 1 2 3 4

10. Anger with my teachers...0 1 2 3 4

11. Anger with my bosses..0 1 2 3 4

12. Anger with police..0 1 2 3 4

13. Anger with government workers 0 1 2 3 4

14. Anger with peers at work...0 1 2 3 4

15. Anger with subordinates at work.....................0 1 2 3 4

16. Anger with customers 0 1 2 3 4

17. Anger with clients..0 1 2 3 4

18. Anger with salespeople...................................0 1 2 3 4

19. Anger with politicians....................................0 1 2 3 4

20. Anger with religious leaders 0 1 2 3 4

21. Anger with God...0 1 2 3 4

22. Anger with strangers 0 1 2 3 4

23. Anger with myself...0 1 2 3 4

24. Anger when waiting in line 0 1 2 3 4

25. Anger when in traffic 0 1 2 3 4

26. Anger with inanimate objects 0 1 2 3 4

27. Anger when I'm being overlooked....................0 1 2 3 4

28. Anger when I'm overcharged 0 1 2 3 4

29. Anger when I'm blamed for somethingI didn't do............0 1 2 3 4

30. Anger when I'm being made fun of................0 1 2 3 4

Now, take a moment to add up your score. The lowest possible score you can get on this inventory is zero. If that happens, you either misunderstood the assignment, weren't honest, or are superhuman. The highest score you can get is 120. If you registered this high, you're a walking volcano ready to erupt.

0—20 The anger you are experiencing is remarkably low. A very low percentage of the population will score this way. You are one of the select few.

21—40 You are substantially more peaceful than the average person.

41—60 You are responding to life's annoyances with an average amount of anger.

61—80 You frequently react in angry ways to life's annoyances. You are substantially more irritable than the average person.

81—120 You win the prize for anger. You are plagued by frequent, intense, and furious reactions that do not quickly disappear. You may be harboring negative feelings long after the initial incident has passed. You may have a reputation for exploding on others. Your blood pressure could be high, or you may be experiencing tension headaches. Your hostile outbursts may be getting you into trouble and damaging relationships. Your anger could be causing much trouble for you at home and at work. Only a small percentage of the adult population reacts as intensely as you do.

Now that you have gotten some idea of the intensity of your anger and where it might be focused, the question arises: Are you happy with what you've found? Anger is a breeding ground for negative and pessimistic attitudes. Do you want to make some changes and deal with your anger? The choice is yours.

Dear God,

It is so easy for me to get angry. I'm impatient and often want people to respond to my needs immediately. I struggle with this emotion when people cut in line, when traffic is slow, and in a host of other situations.

Having strong desires to get even with those who have hurt me or taken advantage of me is nothing new. Neither is holding grudges. Sometimes I just clam up and don't want to talk. Other times I let my venom out on others—usually the people in my own family.

Lord, I'm tired of being angry and having a bad attitude. I'm tired of holding resentments. I'm tired of feeling alone. How desperately I need You to come to my aid. Please help me tame the lion of anger. Help me take responsibility for my thoughts and actions.

Amen.

Attitude Is a Choice...So Pick a Good One.

7

ATTITUDE AND ANGER: PART TWO

*Anybody can become angry, that is easy; but to be angry
with the right person, and to the right degree, and at the right time,
and for the right purpose, and in the right way…that is not easy.*

ARISTOTLE

Kent and Lora were a very angry couple. They fought continually. On one occasion they were visiting Kent's parents when the next event occurred. Kent's parents said something to Lora that upset her greatly, so she proceeded to tell them where they could go in no uncertain terms. Then she slammed the door and walked home.

When Kent finally arrived at home, he yelled at Lora and said, "You can't talk to my parents that way!" Lora then told Kent where he could go also. This angered Kent, and he knocked Lora against the wall. She crumpled to the floor, then got up and ran into the kitchen.

In the process of chasing Lora, Kent slipped on the linoleum floor and fell. Lora grabbed a kitchen knife, put the point of the blade on Kent's throat, and began to press a little. A small amount of blood emerged from the point. She then said, "If you move, you *bleep-bleep-bleep*, I'll kill you!" You'll have to take my word for it, but Lora was quite capable of following through with her threat. It was one of the few times they had complete communication with each other. Her anger and actions were crystal clear.

Anger is a common emotion, although some people struggle with it more than others. Very seldom does anger solve a problem or make a situation better. In rare cases, righteous indignation has helped to end child abuse, spousal beatings, and other social problems; however, this is the exception and not the rule. Most of the anger we experience, or are the recipients of, has negative consequences.

*Anger is an acid that can do more harm to the vessel
in which it is stored than to anything on which it is poured.*

MARK TWAIN

Anger makes difficult situations worse. It sparks aggression, creates health problems, deepens depression, and can cost people their jobs. Anger can lead to divorce, anxiety, guilt, and suicide, and it causes much personal distress and uses up much of our thinking time. Angry individuals have caused property damage by physically expressing their hostility. Many people have lost their lives when deep-seated anger turned to murder.

Can you remember situations when your angry outburst caused personal embarrassment? In general, have your attitude and your anger expressions helped or damaged your relationships? How many people have hurt you with angry comments? How many relationships have been terminated by anger?

To help you get a handle on the emotion of anger, it would be good to keep an anger diary. For the next three weeks, write down any incidents of anger that you experience. Important information to record includes:

- the *people* involved
- the *place* where it occurred
- the *time* of the angry experience
- the *circumstances* surrounding the experience
- the *thoughts* you had about the event after it was over
- your actual *response* at the time (Did you withdraw? Did you attack?)
- the *amount of time* you spent thinking about the situation after it was over

After keeping the anger diary for three weeks, review its contents. Do you notice a recurring theme or topic? Is your anger directed at, or involving, particular individuals? Does your anger occur at a certain time of day or express itself at a particular place? Do you have a consistent response to anger (such as attacking or withdrawing)? Do you spend an inordinate amount of time and energy thinking about anger-producing situations?

The first step in getting a handle on your angry attitude is to understand what is triggering it in your life. Gaining insight and understanding in this area helps you become fully responsible for your actions and thoughts. This creates hope for change, which stimulates motivation, which causes change in thoughts and behavior, which brings about peace and a sense of well-being.

To become proficient in the area of anger management, understanding the anger process is key. The process is comprised of the *event* that triggers the anger, our *mental response*, our *verbal response*, and our *physical response*.

Event

The event is the trigger that sets off the emotion of anger. Perhaps you are late for an appointment and traffic is slow in front of you. Or maybe your spouse makes a comment that hurts you. You may have just spilled something on your clothes or ripped your jacket on a nail. A live, unpleasant event has occurred and caused you irritation.

———— Mental Response ————

When one of these life events occurs, it is helpful to follow the steps below. They will help you control your emotions and reduce your anger attitude.

Get more information before you respond.

It is possible that you may have misunderstood what was said or misinterpreted the situation. This happened to me in Siberia when I was presenting a seminar on character in leadership to a group of military leaders. At one point while I was speaking, I realized the audience had been sitting for a long period of time. I thought it might be good to have them stand and stretch, so I said, "Will you please stand for a moment?" This was translated into Russian, and one of the generals immediately got angry. "You can't tell me to stand!" he said. "You're not a general!"

I was taken aback by his response. He had clearly misunderstood my intention and responded in anger. I had to stop and clarify that I was asking them to stand, stretch, and take a break from the presentation. His anger dissipated when he realized I was not attempting to take control over the generals in the room.

In Proverbs 18:13, wise King Solomon said, "To answer before listening—that is folly and shame" (NIV). The Living Bible translates it this way: "What a shame—yes, how stupid!—to decide before knowing the facts!" It's important to examine all the facts before involving our emotions and responding to others. Proverbs 18:17 says: "Any story sounds true until someone tells the other side and sets the record straight."

Sometimes it's helpful to ask questions like: Could you clarify what you meant? I'm not sure if I quite understand you. Could you rephrase your comment?

Go to the memory file.

Ask yourself if you are experiencing feelings of anger because of what the person is saying or because this person brings someone else to mind. Maybe he or she reminds you of a teacher you once had whom you didn't like. The individual might be speaking in a tone of voice that reminds you of your mother, father, or some other authority figure in your life. Before you respond, be sure you are not dredging up past experiences and loading them onto the person or situation you're presently facing.

Watch out for displaced anger.

Maybe you had a bad day at work after being yelled at by your supervisor. Then, when you get home, you find that your son laid his bicycle on the walkway coming into the house. Do you yell at him? Would you normally yell at your son for such an event? Or are you yelling because you're still upset with your supervisor? Is your lack of patience due to other issues you are dealing with? If so, ask God to help you deal with the *real cause* of anger rather than vent on innocent bystanders.

Evaluate your angry feelings and attitude.

What is causing you to feel the way you do? Did someone say something to hurt you? Were you passed over by someone? Have you experienced some type of loss? Were you embarrassed? Are you dealing with feelings of guilt for something you said or did? Are you feeling threatened? Is too much change going on in your life at this time?

Remind yourself that God is in control.

Nothing catches God off guard. He is not surprised by the events in your life:

> We can rejoice, too, when we run into problems and trials, for we know that they are good for us—they help us learn to be patient. And patience develops strength of character in us and helps us trust God more each time we use it until finally our hope and faith are strong and steady. Then, when that happens, we are able to hold our heads high no matter what happens and know that all is well, for we know how dearly God loves us, and we feel this warm love everywhere within us because God has given us the Holy Spirit to fill our hearts with his love (Romans 5:3-5).

Share your anger with God.

Often King David shared his anger, frustration, and depression with God. The psalms are filled with David's expressions of strong emotion. Some of these feelings are picked up in Psalm 39:1-4. Check it out.

Face the sin of your anger and bad attitude.

Don't pass the buck; don't blame someone else for your anger. Own it, face it, and take responsibility for it. Confess your angry thoughts to God. Ask Him to take away the angry habit patterns that have made deep ruts in your life. Forgive those who have hurt you or have injured you in some fashion. Thank God for bringing situations into your life that help you to develop patience and grow more Christlike. Think about positive things; do not dwell on past hurts and losses.

──── Verbal Response ────

Discipline your mind.

Think about what you are going to say before you open your mouth and start talking. Assess the conflicting issue thoroughly. As you express your thoughts, do not attack the individual with put-downs and harsh words. Attack words do not solve a conflict; they increase it and lock it in.

Don't hold things in for long periods of time.

Often people hold in their hurts and frustrations until they develop into full-blown anger. Instead of dealing with a wastebasket of problems, some people back up a whole dump truck and unload it on the individual they are upset with. No one can deal with that much garbage at once. Remember how to eat an elephant? You eat it one bite at a time. The same is true of problems. Deal with them one at a time, starting with the biggest issue and then tackling the smaller ones.

Don't withdraw into silence.

As I've mentioned, nothing destroys a relationship quicker than silence. Not talking to each other destroys friendships. Ralph Waldo Emerson said: "Go oft to the house of your friend, for weeds soon choke an unused path." Silence begins when someone has been hurt and withdraws. He or she does not want to be hurt anymore. This is understandable, but withdrawing does not solve the problem or reconcile the relationship. It is not easy to crawl out of the cave of silence, but it is absolutely essential if restoration is to occur with the person who hurt you. You need to rise above the conflict and become the reconciler. God will help you do this.

Be open to correction and criticism.

No one likes to be corrected or criticized, and no one wants to admit they are wrong. It's at this point that you may want to argue that someone has hurt you, so you are the victim. This very well may be true, but how are you responding to that hurt? You are not responsible for what others do, but you *are* responsible for your reactions to what others have done. Has your reaction been godly? Have you been responding as Jesus would respond if He were in the same situation?

Share one issue at a time.

When it comes to discussing your hurt or frustration with another individual, deal with only one matter at a time. Don't get sidetracked; stick to the discussion at hand until it's resolved. Don't overload the conversation with too many issues.

Don't use the past against people.

Have you heard about the man who came running into the counselor's office? He said, "You've got to help me. My wife's historical!"

"You mean hysterical," said the counselor.

"No," said the man, "I mean historical. She keeps bring up the past."

The reason we bring up the past is to hurt the people who previously hurt us. It is a form of revenge used to control, guilt, and punish those with whom we have conflicts.

Share your expectations.

A major problem in relationships is when people do not communicate their expectations. Somehow, we think the other person has a crystal ball that will help them know how we are feeling or how we want to be treated. Not only is this unfair to others, but it is not even logical. We only see other people's actions and behaviors; we are not capable of truly understanding their motivations unless they communicate clearly with us. Likewise, other people can't understand us unless we also communicate effectively.

State your hurt or complaint objectively.

When you get to the place where you're sharing your hurts or complaints, do so in a way the other person can understand. Don't let your emotions get out of hand. Discuss the issues in a calm, logical manner.

Share your hurt or complaint in private.

Talking to the other person in private is kind and respectful. People don't like to be reprimanded in public or have their "dirty laundry" hung out for all to see. As Jesus said, "If your brother or sister sins, go and point out their fault, just between the two of you. If they listen to you, you have won them over" (Matthew 18:15 NIV).

Don't threaten to terminate or leave the relationship.

Never precipitate a crisis unless you are willing to face the music. Making threats is not a game to determine who can control the other person. You may have thoughts of terminating the relationship, but do not express those thoughts in words. Don't use this "power play" to compel the other person to conform to your demands, for doing so can cause a great rift in the trust between you. When you threaten to terminate a relationship, you are attempting to hurt the other person. Such maneuvers will turn around and bite you in the rear end.

Don't exaggerate.

State your issues and concerns fairly and truthfully. Don't embellish them or make them bigger than they are. Exaggeration can be used as another form of punishment. It does not help solve the problem; it only increases it.

Allow for reaction time.

You have had the advantage of thinking about the problem or issue for some time. If you press for an answer before the individual has had time to contemplate the issue, you may regret it. Though the other person may respond in the way you want, they may fail to follow through because they are not truly committed to the immediate choice. People get angry when forced into decisions with their backs against the wall. Respect them enough to give them time to think the matter through.

Look for a solution.

Honestly ask yourself: "Am I looking for revenge, or am I looking for a solution?" Looking for solutions is the responsible way to manage angry attitudes.

Physical Response

I've been asked if it's ever right to respond with anger physically. The answer is no—except for extremely rare occasions, such as when you, your family, or your nation is being attacked physically. You may have to respond and become involved physically yourself. I've only had this experience once. It occurred in Los Banos, California.

My daughter and I were walking across a large parking lot when several young men in a car tried to run us down. I barely had enough time to move my daughter out of the way of their car before it reached us.

My instant reaction was one of anger. I instinctively kicked the side door of their car as it went by, which gives you some idea of how close they were to us.

Their reaction was to stop their car about 50 feet ahead of us. Then they opened the doors and started to get out. They were hoping to deal with me personally.

I had a different thought in mind, so I started running—*toward* their car as fast as I could. I didn't care how many were in the car. They had just attacked my family with a large, heavy, deadly weapon.

The driver then saw me running directly at him and pulled his foot back in the car. The others also got back into the car and pulled away just before I reached them. Then, in their great show of bravery, they yelled swear words out the windows and gave me the finger as they drove off.

Most physical anger takes place because the individuals don't have the communication skills to deal with the problem verbally or mentally. People who inflict physical injury on others are trying to control situations that have gotten out of hand for them. They do it in the only way they know how: with violence. They may also be motivated by desires to hurt the other person, get revenge, or prove to them who the boss is. Whatever the motivation, violence brings devastation to relationships and amplifies the problem.

If you're dealing with anger in a physical manner, you need immediate help. Admit you have a problem and seek assistance before someone is physically harmed, emotionally damaged, or killed because of your temper. This is not a situation where you can say, "I'll work out the problem myself." Be courageous enough to seek help.

Flying off the handle sometimes causes hammers and humans to lose their heads, as well as their effectiveness.

WILLIAM ARTHUR WARD

—— Homework Assignment ——

Have you ever wondered what God thinks about human anger? Take a moment to open your Bible and review a dozen thoughts about this powerful emotion.

Psalm 37:8	Proverbs 22:24	Ephesians 4:31
Proverbs 14:29	Proverbs 29:22	Colossians 3:8
Proverbs 15:1	Ecclesiastes 7:9	1 Timothy 2:8
Proverbs 15:18	Ephesians 4:26	James 1:19-20

Dear God,

Please help me to get rid of the acid of anger in my life. I don't need it eating away at my thoughts and emotions or destroying the lives of others. Assist me in becoming aware of my tendency to dwell on my perceived hurts in life. Help me to move away from the negative thoughts and dwell on positive thoughts. Please help me guard my mouth so I won't spew destructive words and destroy the spirits of my family, friends, and coworkers. Help me to put into practice Your wisdom about anger as is suggested in the Bible. Transform the energy I'm giving to hurt and anger so I can use that energy to help others.

Amen.

Attitude Is a Choice...So Pick a Good One.

8

ATTITUDE AND TEMPERAMENT

Behavior is the mirror in which everyone shows their image.

JOHANN WOLFGANG VON GOETHE

'm fed up. I'm angry at Sally and mad at myself. You would think that I'd learn...but not me. I keep opening myself up to more hurt." Cindy continued to pour out her hurt and anger to her husband.

"I don't think Sally tried to hurt you deliberately," he responded sympathetically. "She just likes to talk a lot."

"That's for sure!" Cindy retorted. "You tell Sally and you tell the world. Why can't she keep a secret? I thought she was my best friend."

Picky, Picky, Picky

"You can't do anything to please my boss," Carlos complained. "I worked all week on the Carter project, and he didn't even say thanks. All he did was point out four misspelled words in the report. I don't know if I can keep on working for such a narrow-minded, critical perfectionist."

You Could Make a Fortune Renting Your Head Out as a Balloon

"When are you going to start thinking? I swear, if brains were dynamite, you wouldn't have enough to blow your nose."

It wasn't the first time Janet had heard words like these from her father. She was criticized almost every time she asked him to help her with her schoolwork. He would sometimes rant and rave at her for over 20 minutes. She was torn between the need for help and the fear of the tirade her dad would start. Janet wondered how much more verbal abuse she could take.

King for a Day

"I'm sick and tired of Frank's pushiness," Jeff complained. "He orders everyone around. Who made him king anyway? He's no better than the rest of us. One of these days I'm going to let him have it."

If you are alive, you'll experience conflicts with people. Your conflicts may be with family members, schoolmates, coworkers, friends, or even strangers. It's not easy getting along with some people. But who said it would be? We were never promised smooth sailing when it comes to human relationships. Getting along with others takes effort. It means loving people when we don't feel like it and when they are not very lovable.

However, this book was not primarily designed to help you learn how to get along with others (although such a book would be helpful). This book is about how you can make changes in your attitude. When you make changes in your attitude, other people will have an easier time getting along with you.

With that thought in mind, let's take a look at your temperament and social style. What hindrances, if any, are the results of a poor attitude or behavior on your part?

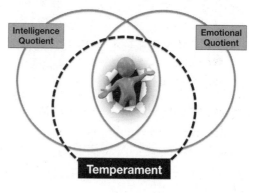

Intelligence, Emotions, & Temperament

Intelligence Quotient

Emotional Quotient

Temperament

Intelligence Quotient (IQ)—a measure of a person's reasoning ability as indicated by an intelligence test; the ratio of a person's mental age to their chronological age.

Emotional Quotient (EQ)—the level of one's ability to understand oneself, other people, what motivates others, and how to work cooperatively with them; involves self-awareness, self-regulation, motivation, empathy, and social skills.

Temperament—sometimes referred to as *social style*; refers to one's natural and habitual inclinations inherited at birth. This includes behavior tendencies, manner of thinking, and emotional responses that express themselves in customary moods or reactions to events. Temperament is sometimes referred to as disposition, pattern of innate characteristics, or attitude. It's basically one's behavioral approach to the world. Temperament behavior can be noticed early in babies. For example, some babies seem relaxed and very cuddly. Parents react by holding them a lot and talking to them. Other babies seem to be very active, and parents are not quite sure how to deal with their child's constant movement. What they don't realize is that these babies need motion. They respond to tickling, change of position, or mild tossing in the air.

Personality—how one individually *expresses* inherited temperament or social style; can be affected by upbringing and environment.

Character—the *quality* of one's individual personality; affected by morals, values, and ethics.

When it comes to temperament or social styles, the important thing is to focus on actual behavior and not on the intention or motivation behind the behavior. We only see the actions of people, and other people only see our actions. John Locke suggested, "The actions of men are the best interpreters of their thoughts." What we don't see in other people are their:

Ambitions	Dreams	Likes
Attitudes	Expectations	Perceptions
Beliefs	Feelings	Thoughts
Dislikes	Hurts	Values

Behaviors can be classified into large groupings. For example:

- good and bad behavior
- active and passive behavior
- sowing and reaping behavior
- optimistic and pessimistic behavior
- task-oriented behavior and relationship-oriented behavior
- assertive behavior and nonassertive behavior

When it comes to temperament, there are four basic social styles: analytical, driver, amiable, and expressive. To understand your particular social style, it's important to determine if you lean toward attitudes and behaviors that are more *asking* or more *telling* in social interactions.

In the chart below, place a check mark next to the phrases you think best describe the behaviors and attitudes you *most often* display when dealing with people and events in your life. You may find that some characteristics in both lists describe you. Most people will discover that they have more checks on one side than the other. This will give you a clue about how your attitude is tied to your behavior.

ASK CHARACTERISTICS	TELL CHARACTERISTICS
☐ Less assertive, more introverted	☐ More assertive, more extroverted
☐ Outward response under stress: flight	☐ Outward response under stress: fight
☐ Driving emotion and motivation under stress: fear	☐ Driving emotion and motivation under stress: anger
☐ Communicates hesitantly	☐ Readily communicative
☐ Lower quantity of talk	☐ Higher quantity of talk
☐ Pace of speech: slower	☐ Pace of speech: fast
☐ Speech volume: soft	☐ Speech volume: loud
☐ Body movements: slow and deliberate	☐ Body movements: fast and rapid
☐ More tentative and less forceful	☐ Less tentative and more forceful
☐ Reserves opinions	☐ Shares opinions easily
☐ Less confrontational	☐ More confrontational
☐ Nonaggressive	☐ More aggressive
☐ Makes thoughtful decisions	☐ More decisive
☐ Will not pressure others for decisions	☐ Will pressure others for decisions
☐ Patient	☐ Impatient
☐ Not a huge risk taker	☐ More of a risk taker
☐ Avoids the use of power if at all possible	☐ Will use personal and positional power
☐ Attentive listener	☐ Has difficulty listening

Merrill and Reid, *Personal Styles and Effective Performance*; Robert Bolton and Dorothy G. Bolton, *Social Style/Management Style*, adapted.

Which one are you?   ☐ Asker   ☐ Teller

The next step is to determine if you tend to be more task-oriented or relationship-oriented. Again, place a check next to the phrases you think best describe the behaviors and attitudes you *most often* display when dealing with people and events in your life.

TASK CHARACTERISTICS	REALTIONSHIP CHARACTERISTICS
☐ Dress: more formal	☐ Dress: more informal
☐ Topics of speech: current issues and tasks at hand	☐ Topics of speech: people, stories, and anecdotes
☐ Body posture: more rigid	☐ Body posture: more relaxed
☐ Facial expressions: more controlled	☐ Facial expressions: more animated
☐ General attitude: toward the serious side	☐ General attitude: toward the playful side
☐ Reserved	☐ Outgoing
☐ Controlled and guarded emotions	☐ Free to share emotions
☐ Filled with facts and data	☐ Filled with opinions and stories
☐ Less interested in small talk	☐ More interested in small talk
☐ Decisions are fact-based	☐ Decisions are feeling-or "gut"-based
☐ Disciplined about time	☐ Less disciplined about time
☐ Strict and disciplined about rules	☐ Permissive and lenient about rules
☐ Restrained and guarded when sharing opinions	☐ Impulsive and forceful when sharing opinions
☐ Hard to get to know; keeps distance from others	☐ Easy to get to know; does not keep distance from others
☐ Preoccupied	☐ Carefree

Merrill and Reid, *Personal Styles and Effective Performance*; Robert Bolton and Dorothy G. Bolton, *Social Style/Management Style,* adapted.

Which portrays you best?
☐ Task-oriented ☐ Relationship-oriented

Which of the Four Words Best Describes You?
☐ Analytical ☐ Driver ☐ Amiable ☐ Expressive

All temperament or social styles have their good and bad points. Listed below are positive and negative attitudes and behaviors that each of the social styles display at various times. Their displays depend on mindset, attitude, and the events or circumstances.

Strengths and Weaknesses

Circle the words—both positive and negative—that best describe your attitude and behavior.

ANALYTICAL		DRIVER	
NEGATIVE	POSITIVE	NEGATIVE	POSITIVE
Moody	Industrious	Unsympathetic	Determined
Critical	Gifted	Pushy	Independent
Negative	Perfectionist	Insensitive	Productive
Rigid	Persistent	Inconsiderate	Strong-willed
Indecisive	Conscientious	Severe	Visionary
Legalistic	Loyal	Hostile	Optimistic
Self-centered	Serious	Sarcastic	Active
Stuffy	Aesthetic	Tough	Practical
Touchy	Idealistic	Unforgiving	Courageous
Vengeful	Exacting	Domineering	Decisive
Picky	Sensitive	Opinionated	Self-confident
Persecution-prone	Self-sacrificing	Prejudiced	Efficient
Unsociable	Orderly	Harsh	Leader
Moralistic	Self-disciplined	Proud	
Theoretical			

AMIABLE		EXPRESSIVE	
NEGATIVE	POSITIVE	NEGATIVE	POSITIVE
Unbothered	Calm	Weak-willed	Outgoing
Conforming	Supportive	Manipulative	Ambitious
Blasé	Easygoing	Restless	Charismatic
Indolent	Likeable	Disorganized	Warm
Unsure	Respectful	Unproductive	Stimulating
Spectating	Diplomatic	Excitable	Responsive
Selfish	Efficient	Undependable	Talkative
Ingratiating	Willing	Undisciplined	Enthusiastic
Stingy	Organized	Obnoxious	Carefree
Stubborn	Conservative	Loud	Compassionate
Dependent	Practical	Reactive	Dramatic
Self-protective	Dependable	Exaggerating	Generous
Indecisive	Reluctant to lead	Fearful	Friendly
Awkward	Agreeable	Egotistical	
Fearful	Humorous (dry)		

Homework

Take a few moments to review the boxes you checked and the words you circled. How do you feel about the items you selected? Are you happy with them, or are you somewhat disappointed?

Take a piece of paper and write down the positive words or phrases you selected in one column. Then copy down the negative words or phrases you selected in another. Next, circle five of the most positive words or phrases you selected. Then circle five of the most negative words or phrases you selected.

These ten items are your homework for the next three weeks. Take a three-by-five-inch index card and write the five positive descriptors on one side and the five negative descriptors on the other side of the card. Carry the card with you, and look at it at least three times every day. You can set an alarm on your phone to remind you. Endeavor to enhance and reinforce the five positive words or phrases during the next three weeks. At the same time, attempt to modify or eliminate the negative characteristics you selected.

You may be saying, "This is going to take some effort!" You've got that right. If the ten items you write on the card are important to you, you'll do it. If they are not important to you, you will carry on with your present attitudes and behavior. You see, attitude is a choice. Which version of yourself do you want to be?

If you want to change attitudes, start with a change in behavior.

KATHARINE HEPBURN

Dear God,

Wow! These are some new thoughts about how my temperament and social style can affect my attitude in a positive or negative way. Help me to become more aware of my own behavior and how it can hinder relationships. I need to work on the positive traits so You will be happier with me and I will be happier with myself. I need You to help me face the negative issues in my life. Give me the courage and strength to change. Help me to understand that my attitude and behavior are mirrors of what is going on inside of me. Help me to use the three-by-five-inch card to keep me on track. I want to choose a happy attitude.

Amen.

Attitude Is a Choice...So Pick a Good One.

9

ATTITUDE AND HABITS

Good habits are hard to develop but easy to live with; bad habits are easy to develop but hard to live with. The habits you have and the habits that have you will determine almost everything you achieve or fail to achieve.

Brian Tracy

first met Harrison at a party. I didn't know him personally, but I could hear him distinctly. His voice was loud and very demanding. As I turned his direction, I could see he was a big man who towered above the other men by about six inches. He was in a heated discussion about politics and religious faith. His demeanor was strong, challenging, and argumentative. It looked like he was winning because all the other men finally grew quiet.

A little later I had the opportunity to talk with him myself. We introduced ourselves, and I said, "It looked like you were in a pretty heated discussion earlier."

"Yeah, sometimes I get a little carried away. I guess it's my upbringing. We came from a family that held strong opinions and yelled a lot."

"I heard you mention that you're a Christian. Do you come on that strong with everyone?"

"What do you mean by that?" he replied. I could see him tensing up, and he fixed me with a challenging look.

"I mean you sounded pretty angry, and I was wondering if that's a pattern for you. Do you think being angry helps or hurts your example as a Christian?"

"That's just the way I am," he said with some intensity and a tinge of hostility.

I smiled. "I think it would be more appropriate to say that's the way you've chosen to be," I said. "You could choose to speak in a kinder and gentler manner if you wanted to. It sounds more like your argumentativeness is a habit pattern."

Our character is basically a composite of our habits.
Because they are consistent, often unconscious patterns,
they constantly, daily, express our character.

STEPHEN COVEY

Paul the apostle addresses this subject in Titus 3. He says "not to speak evil of any man," and that believers "must not be argumentative but gentle, showing themselves agreeable to everybody" (verse 2 PHILLIPS). The chapter goes on, telling us to "steer clear of stupid arguments, genealogies, controversies and quarrels over the Law. They settle nothing and lead nowhere. If a man is still argumentative after the second warning you should reject him. You can be sure that he has a moral twist, and he knows it" (verses 8-11 PHILLIPS).

Your personality is made up, developed, and comprised of three basic elements:

1. Your God-given physical body

2. Your environment (where you were raised and how you were nurtured)

3. Your acquired habits of thinking, speaking, and behaving

Harrison had developed a habit of argumentativeness. He didn't take responsibility for his personal behavior. He excused himself and his behavior by blaming his family of origin for his coming on strong and for being "in the face" of other people. "It's just the way I am," he claimed—which subtly suggested he was not about to change.

A great portion of your life involves habit patterns that are comfortable and familiar for you. According to researchers at Duke University, habits account for about 40 percent of our behaviors on a given day.[2]

Habits are automatic and are exhibited without conscious thought.

For example:

- What side of the bed do you usually get out of in the morning?
- Which leg do you first put into a pair of pants you're going to wear?
- Do you button your shirt from the top down or from the bottom up?
- Do you need a cup of coffee to start your day? Or something else?
- Do you drive the same route to work every day?

Other habits include:

- Being a follower
- Being a leader
- Reading the Bible
- Body language
- Brushing teeth
- Church activities
- Combing hair
- Driving patterns
- Exercise routine
- Gossiping
- How much you smile
- Putting on makeup
- Shaving
- Spending money
- Taking medicine
- Spending time with kids
- Bedtime
- Tone of voice
- Using credit cards
- Word choices
- Worrying
- Posture

Some people say they can't change their personality. Remember, part of your personality is your acquired habits of thinking, speaking, and behaving. You *can* change those things.

For example, let's say Harrison is amid a heavy argument with his wife, Shelbie. They're calling each other names. They're not the least bit happy with each other.

All of a sudden, I show up at the door and tell them to stop arguing with each other. I go on to suggest they should be happy and plan for their future. What do you think will be their response? Who knows? They might tell me where I should go in no uncertain terms.

Let's reimagine the scenario. Harrison and Shelbie are still in a heated discussion when the doorbell rings. Harrison opens the door, and three strangers are standing on his porch with a sign in their hands. Shelbie wanders up to see who's there. Then the three strangers shout together: "Congratulations! You just won the Publishers Clearinghouse Sweepstakes—meaning you've won $14,000 a week for life!"

Do you think it might be possible for Harrison and Shelbie to change their thoughts, attitudes, and behavior?

> *Excellence is an art won by training and habituation: we do*
> *not act rightly because we have virtue or excellence, but we*
> *rather have these because we have acted rightly... we are what*
> *we repeatedly do. Excellence, then, is not an act but a habit.*
>
> ARISTOTLE

When Judy first came for counseling, she was severely depressed. She didn't have any motivation to do normal housework or even go shopping with friends. She broke into tears easily and sometimes spoke in angry tones.

Judy and her mother had not spoken to each other for the last three months. They had been in an off-and-on battle since she was a teenager. After she married Rick and had their first child, the tension between Judy and her mom progressed. Her mother continually told her how to take care of the baby and how to clean house. Judy was sick and tired of the whole mess.

Rick, too, was tired of all the raw emotions. He had listened to Judy's complaints until he could stand it no longer. He began to tell Judy to grow up and get over it. This did not help their marital adjustment.

Judy had come to a place where the pain was so great she did not know what to do. She was angry with her mother, angry with Rick, angry with God, and angry with herself. She was hurting so much that unless she changed, she worried she might do something drastic. She had been contemplating escaping the pain through suicide.

After several sessions, she realized she needed to make peace with her pain and peace with others. Her anger was destroying her, and she knew it. The hardest hurdle for her to jump over was forgiving her mother. This was no easy task, and it took her several weeks to muster up the courage to do it.

We talked about what she would like to achieve and how to get there, as well as motivation and how to take positive steps forward. I shared that there are two ways to get started. One is to begin dealing with small issues in life—for her, this meant cleaning her house, ironing, and helping neighbors. Victory in small areas would give her motivation to overcome larger areas of difficulty.

The other method for getting started is to deal with larger issues before tackling the smaller issues. For Judy, this meant going to her mother, admitting her anger, and asking for forgiveness. This would be hard, but afterward, everything else would be easier to conquer. She would be on a downhill run, increasing the speed of change.

Either method works. Remember this question: "How do you eat an elephant?" The answer is still: "One bite at a time." Change does not happen all at once. Life is a continuing process of growth through struggles.

More powerful than the will to win, is the courage
to begin. He who steps out the door already has
a good part of his journey behind him.

UNKNOWN

Judy had to consider the paths of small-to-big or big-to-small for some time. She chose to take the faster route. She went for the big first and went directly to her mother, then felt a real sense of freedom and release when she finally forgave her mother. Her next battle was to forgive herself for her anger at God and at Rick. When this was accomplished, a great fear overcame her. She was afraid she would fall back into the same old patterns of anger and resentment. She knew she had to set up a plan to change her old habits and style of behavior. Choosing to do the right thing is not always easy; sometimes it involves a battle.

Paul the apostle refers to this battle in Romans 7:

I don't really understand myself, for I want to do what is right, but I don't do it. Instead, I do what I hate. But if I know that what I am doing is wrong, this shows that I agree that the law is good. So I am not the one doing wrong; it is sin living in me that does it. And I know that nothing good lives in me, that is, in my sinful nature. I want to do what is right, but I can't. I want to do what is good, but I don't. I don't want to do what is wrong, but I do it anyway. But if I do what I don't want to do, I am not really the one doing wrong; it is sin living in me that does it...

I have discovered this principle of life—that when I want to do what is right, I inevitably do what is wrong. I love God's law with all my heart. But there is another power within me that is at war with my mind. This power makes me a slave to the sin that is still within me. Oh, what a miserable person I am! Who will free me from this life that is dominated by sin and death? Thank God! The answer is in Jesus Christ our Lord. So you see how it is: In my mind I really want to obey God's law, but because of my sinful nature I am a slave to sin (verses 15-17, 21-25 NLT).

How do we make *lasting change* in bad habits and attitudes of thinking, speaking, and behaving? Let me ask this question: When is a liar not a liar, and when is a thief not a thief? One quick answer is when they stop lying and they stop stealing.

That said, does just stopping something mean real change has happened in a person's life? A thief might stop stealing momentarily for the fear of being caught. The liar may stop lying for a period of time because their deception may be discovered. Just stopping any habit for a moment does not mean lasting change is taking place.

Lasting change comes when you *stop* doing negative and sinful things and *start* doing positive and godly things. Bad behavior must end and be replaced by good behavior.

Let's come back to the liar. In Ephesians 4:25 we read, "Stop lying to each other; tell the truth, for we are parts of each other and when we lie to each other we are hurting ourselves." When is a liar no longer a liar? When they start telling the truth.

With regard to the thief, Ephesians 4:28 states, "If anyone is stealing he must stop it and begin using those hands of his for honest work so he can give to others in need." When is a thief no longer a thief? When they start doing honest work.

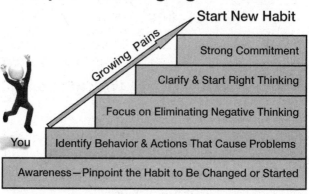

Steps to Changing Attitude

What follows are some areas where lasting change can occur if one puts off negative attitudes and behaviors and puts on positive attitudes and behaviors. The putting off and putting on process is not an easy task. It's like any habit; it takes time and effort to establish, and it takes time and effort to change. Change demands a strong commitment.

Do you remember the first time you tried to roller-skate or ice-skate? What happened? Were your ankles a little wobbly? Did you feel uncomfortable? Did you fall down? Did you feel embarrassed in front of others? Did you feel like quitting because you were not immediately successful?

> *A nail is driven out by another nail.*
> *Habit is overcome by habit.*
>
> DESIDERIUS ERASMUS

How do you develop a new habit or skill? With repetition over time. Everyone goes through the same learning process. You will experience some successes and some failures along the way. Professional athletes do not become professional overnight; they practice and practice.

PUT OFF	PUT ON	PUT OFF	PUT ON
Selfishness	→Love	Pride	→Humility
Carelessness	→Alertness	Idleness	→Initiative
Distraction	→Attentiveness	Self-Pity	→Joyfulness
Fearfulness	→Boldness	Infidelity	→Loyalty
Rashness	→Cautiousness	Anger	→Peace
Indifference	→Compassion	Willfulness	→Obedience
Covetousness	→Contentment	Confusion	→Orderliness
Double-Mindedness	→Decisiveness	Restlessness	→Patience
Inconsistency	→Dependability	Contentiousness	→Persuasiveness
Faintheartedness	→Determination	Tardiness	→Punctuality
Slothfulness	→Diligence	Wastefulness	→Resourcefulness
Discouragement	→Endurance	Unreliability	→Responsibility
Apathy	→Enthusiasm	Anxiety	→Security
Unbelief	→Faith	Self-Indulgence	→Self-Control
Resistance	→Flexibility	Callousness	→Sensitivity
Bitterness	→Forgiveness	Hypocrisy	→Sincerity
Stinginess	→Generosity	Incompleteness	→Thoroughness
Harshness	→Gentleness	Extravagance	→Thriftiness
Murmuring	→Gratefulness	Condemnation	→Tolerance
Disrespect	→Honor	Deception	→Truthfulness

> *Do something every day that you don't want*
> *to do. This is the golden rule for acquiring the*
> *habit of doing your duty without pain.*
>
> MARK TWAIN

One of the big factors in changing lifestyles and relationships is procrastination. The word comes from the Latin *pro*, which means forward motion, and *crastinus*, which means belonging to tomorrow. Procrastination is putting off something burdensome or unpleasant, to avoid doing something you know you really should do. It is the belief that taking action would be more painful than putting it off.

We all tend to avoid pain. We want guarantees that everything will be all right. We tell ourselves that we will wait for the "magical moment"— when the time is just right. We engage in wishful thinking. Some of us even deserve a gold medal for how well we procrastinate. Gloria Pitzer said it this way:

> Procrastination is my sin. It brings me naught but sorrow. I know that I should stop it. In fact, I will—tomorrow!

We sometimes think to ourselves: *If I only had more time. If I only had more money. If I had a more secure job. I'll wait until I feel better. I'll do it tomorrow.* Little do we realize that when we postpone action, things can get worse. We get older. We put on more weight. We become unhealthy and out of shape. As we spin our wheels, we dig deeper holes in our emotions and deeper ruts in our habits. We think, *I can always quit. I have the strength to do this; I just don't want to.*

> *Putting off an easy thing makes it hard, and*
> *putting off a hard one makes it impossible.*
>
> GEORGE HORACE LORIMER

—— **Possible Habit Areas to Be** ——
Considered for Change

Alcohol	Broken Relationships
Argumentative Attitude	Caffeine Addiction
Bitterness	Chewing Fingernails
Boredom	Cracking Knuckles

Cracking Neck
Critical Spirit
Disloyalty
Doubts
Drugs
Eatig Disorder
Envy
Extramarital Affair
Fantasies
Fears
Fidgeting
Finger Tapping
Forgetfulness
Gambling
Gluttony
Gossip
Gum Snapping
Hair Pulling
Hatefulness
Jaw Clenching
Jealousy
Knee Jiggling

Lack of Commitment
Laziness
Lip Biting
Living in the Past
Lying
Not Keeping Secrets
Obsessiveness
Pessimism
Promise Breaking
Rapid Eating
Rebellion
Regret
Resentment
Sexual Problems
Sloppiness
Smoking
Snacking
Stealing
Swearing
Tics
Toe Tapping
Worrying

Questions and Plans for Desired Changes

1. **Who:** I am struggling with the following people at this time in my life:

_____

_____

2. **What:** I am presently struggling with the following issues or bad habits:

_____

_____

3. **Where:** The location where most of these struggles take place is:

_____

_____

4. **When:** These struggles usually appear at this time of day, month, or season:

_____

_____

5. **Why:** I have allowed these struggles to overwhelm me because:

_____

_____

6. **How:** The things that contribute to my struggles are:

_____

_____

7. I would like to see the following changes take place:

_____

_____

8. I need to forgive the following people:

_____

_____

9. I need to confront the following people or behaviors:

_____

_____

10. The first thing I plan to do is:

_____

_____

11. The second thing I plan to do is:

_____

_____

12. My commitment to begin this change is on this date and
    this place:

_____

_____

Robin Sieger in his book *42 Days to Wealth, Health, and Happiness* suggests that it takes 42 days to establish patterns of behavior, and about another three weeks to lock in the habit pattern. This means if you are serious and consistent for about 63 days, you can break or do away with negative habits or establish brand-new habits and attitudes.

For example, let's take smoking. When a person smokes their first cigarette, it's not a pleasant experience. When inhaling for the first time, you cough and choke, and your body rebels at having smoke in its lungs.

Only by repeated attempts do you learn how to bring smoke into your body without coughing. Why would someone keep up this type of behavior? Because there's a *reward*. Smoking could help you feel accepted by a group. You may think it's cool. Or you may like the physical effects of nicotine. Regardless of the motivation, by smoking for six weeks, you can establish a smoking habit that may control you for a long time.

Once you decide to start a habit—or decide to break a habit (regardless of what it may be)—you need about three weeks (21 days) of repeating the habit before it becomes consistent and familiar. Add another three weeks (42 days total), and you can establish a habit pattern. Then add another three weeks (63 days total), and you will most likely lock in the habit pattern.

The critical time is the first three weeks. This is when you "struggle" with either starting or abandoning a habit pattern. If you want to break bad habits, you need three weeks of consistency. Don't give up. Work hard at learning a new way of thinking and behaving. The same is true for starting good habits. Determine to be diligent on the way toward positive change.

Ask God to help you during the process of change and the establishment of a new lifestyle. He understands and wants to give you the support and courage to follow through.

> *Since he himself has now been through suffering and temptation, he knows what it is like when we suffer and are tempted, and he is wonderfully able to help us.*
>
> HEBREWS 2:18

> *Repetition of the same thought or physical action develops into a habit which, repeated frequently enough, becomes an automatic reflex.*
>
> NORMAN VINCENT PEALE

Dear God,

I've been feeling pain and discouragement for a long time. I have been overpowered by critical and negative thoughts. My pessimistic thinking has worn a deep rut in my mind, and I don't think I can climb out of the rut by myself. Please help me. I want to see new vistas instead of the bottom of this ditch I'm in. I want to take the plunge into a new way of thinking and living. I need a new attitude and the determination to break bad habits and start good habits. Please wash my mind with new thoughts. I want to change how I've been viewing my problems. I'm going to need Your help and strength. Please encourage me with the commitment and determination to continue—not just for 42 days, but for more than 63 days. I want the changes to be permanent. I can hardly wait to see what You're going to do!

Amen.

Attitude Is a Choice...So Pick a Good One.

10

ATTITUDE AND ADVERSITY

Search for the seed of good in every adversity. Master that
principle and you will own a precious shield that will guard
you well through all the darkest valleys you must traverse. Stars
may be seen from the bottom of a deep well, when they cannot
be discerned from the mountaintop. So will you learn things
in adversity that you would never have discovered without
trouble. There is always a seed of good. Find it and prosper.

OG MANDINO

You know it's going to be a bad day when:

- Your horn sticks on the freeway behind 32 Hell's Angels
- Your birthday cake collapses from the weight of the candles
- Your twin sister forgets your birthday
- You need one bathroom scale for each foot
- Your doctor tells you that you are allergic to chocolate chip cookies
- People think you are 60…and you really are
- Everyone is laughing at you instead of with you

Mark it down. Everyone has adversity in life. The only difference is the degree of adversity between people. According to the Centers for Disease Control, 61 percent of all adults have had at least one adverse childhood experience (also referred to as an ACE), and 16 percent have experienced four or more traumatic events. Are you one of the 61 percent? Key adverse experiences include:

Abandonment	Disability
Chronic Pain	Emotional Abuse
Death of a Parent	Extreme Bullying

Major Illness	Sexual Abuse
Mental Abuse	Social Rejection
Physical Abuse	Spiritual Manipulation
Poverty	Victim of Divorce

The dictionary defines *adversity* as a state or instance of serious or continued difficulty or misfortune. Hurts, regrets, shyness, loneliness, worries, anxieties, unfairness, job loss, relational difficulties, unfulfilled expectations, guilt, low self-image, and many other problems can be considered adversities.

Does Adversity
Have You on Your Back?

When life takes the wind out of your
sails, it is to test you at the oars.

ROBERT BREAULT

Get More Information

Dealing with adversity in life begins with getting a clear picture of what's going on. We must collect as much information as possible because a doctor cannot treat a problem without a diagnosis.

We've already discussed Proverbs 18:13, but here is a refresher: "He that answereth a matter before he heareth it, it is folly and shame unto him" (KJV). Put another way: "What a shame—yes, how stupid!—to decide before knowing the facts!"

Thank God for Adversity

James 1:2 says:

> Dear brothers, is your life full of difficulties and temptations? Then be happy, for when the way is rough, your patience has a chance to grow.

John C. Maxwell says:

> It's easy to have a great attitude when things are going our way...It's when difficult challenges rise before us, and the attitude within us...becomes the difference-maker.

Identify the Cause of Pain and Adversity

- Emotional Pain
- Financial Pain
- Mental Pain
- Physical Pain
- Social Pain
- Spiritual Pain
- Vocational Pain
- Pain of Fear
- Pain of Anger
- Pain of Loss and Grief
- Pain of the Unknown
- Pain of Change

> *Is the pain and suffering a problem that we can work on, or is it a fact of life that we have to accept, make peace with, and learn to live with?*
>
> R.E. PHILLIPS

Is the Adversity You Face Something That Will Strengthen You?

Romans 5:3-5 says:

> We can rejoice, too, when we run into problems and trials, for we know that they are good for us—they help us learn to be patient. And patience develops strength of character in us and helps us trust God more each time we use it until

finally our hope and faith are strong and steady. Then, when that happens, we are able to hold our heads high no matter what happens and know that all is well, for we know how dearly God loves us, and we feel this warm love everywhere within us because God has given us the Holy Spirit to fill our hearts with his love.

Charles Stanley also has thoughts on the purpose of adversity. According to him:

Adversity is not simply a tool. It is God's most effective tool for the advancement of our spiritual lives. The circumstances and events that we see as setbacks are oftentimes the very things that launch us into periods of intense spiritual growth. Once we begin to understand this, and accept it as a spiritual fact of life, adversity becomes easier to bear.

Is the Adversity You Face Something That Will Help to Mature You?

James 1:2-8 says:

Dear brothers, is your life full of difficulties and temptations? Then be happy, for when the way is rough, your patience has a chance to grow. So let it grow, and don't try to squirm out of your problems. For when your patience is finally in full bloom, then you will be ready for anything, strong in character, full and complete. If you want to know what God wants you to do, ask him, and he will gladly tell you, for he is always ready to give a bountiful supply of wisdom to all who ask him; he will not resent it. But when you ask him, be sure that you really expect him to tell you, for a doubtful mind will be as unsettled as a wave of the sea that is driven and tossed by the wind; and every decision you then make will be uncertain, as you turn first this way and then that. If you don't ask with faith, don't expect the Lord to give you any solid answer.

During the seventeenth century, François Fénelon wrote about dealing with problems, trials, and adversity. He referred to adversity as a cross to bear.

> So we must learn to bear all suffering with composure, even those which come upon us through no fault of our own. But we must beware of that restlessness of spirit which might be our own fault. We can add to our God-given cross by agitated resistance and an unwillingness to suffer.

He goes on to suggest how a change of attitude can change your view of adversity.

> A cross which comes from God ought to be welcomed without any concern for self. And when you accept your cross this way, even though it is painful, you will find that you can bear it in peace. But when you receive your cross unwillingly, you will find it to be doubly severe. The resistance within is harder to bear than the cross itself. But if you recognize the hand of God, and make no opposition to His Will, you will have peace in the midst of affliction. Happy indeed are they who can bear their sufferings with this simple peace and perfect submission to the will of God! Nothing so shortens and soothes suffering as this spirit of non-resistance.[3]

Keep in mind that the world is full of suffering. If you forget that— all you have to do is turn on the nightly news and be reminded of that fact. We cannot always escape suffering. Sometimes the only course is to endure it and go straight through it.

Is the Adversity You Face Something That Will Turn to Gold?

According to 1 Peter 1:6-9:

> So be truly glad! There is wonderful joy ahead, even though the going is rough for a while down here. These trials are only to test your faith, to see whether or not it is strong and

pure. It is being tested as fire tests gold and purifies it—and your faith is far more precious to God than mere gold; so if your faith remains strong after being tried in the test tube of fiery trials, it will bring you much praise and glory and honor on the day of his return. You love him even though you have never seen him; though not seeing him, you trust him; and even now you are happy with the inexpressible joy that comes from heaven itself. And your further reward for trusting him will be the salvation of your souls.

GOLD IN THE FIRE

He sat by a fire of sevenfold heat
As He watched by the precious ore,
And closer He bent with a searching gaze
As He heated it more and more.
He knew He had ore that could stand the test,
And He wanted the finest gold
To mold as a crown for the King to wear,
Set with gems with price untold.
So He laid our gold in the burning fire,
Tho' we fain would have said to Him, "Nay,"
And He watched the dross that we had not seen,
And it melted and passed away.
And the gold grew brighter and yet more bright,
But our eyes were so dim with tears.
We saw but the fire—not the Master's hand,
And questioned it with anxious fears.
Yet our gold shone out with a richer glow,
As it mirrored a form above,
That bent o'er the fire, tho' unseen by us,
With a look of ineffable love.
Can we think that it pleases His loving heart
To cause us a moment's pain?
Ah, no! But He saw through the present cross

The bliss of eternal gain.
So He waited there with a watchful eye,
With a love that is strong and sure,
And His gold did not suffer a bit more heat,
Than was needed to make it pure.

AUTHOR UNKNOWN

If finding God's way in the suddenness of storms makes
our faith grow broad, then trusting God's wisdom in
the "dailyness" of living makes it grow deep. And strong.
Whatever may be your circumstances— however long it
may have lasted—wherever you may be today, I bring
this reminder: The stronger the winds, the deeper the roots,
and the longer the winds…the more beautiful the tree.

CHARLES SWINDOLL

Will the Adversity You're Facing Help You to Focus on God's Will?

According to 1 Peter 4:1-2:

> Since Christ suffered and underwent pain, you must have the same attitude he did; you must be ready to suffer, too. For remember, when your body suffers, sin loses its power, and you won't be spending the rest of your life chasing after evil desires but will be anxious to do the will of God.

Elisabeth Kübler-Ross talks about individuals who have encountered deep grief over the death of loved ones and other difficulties in life:

> The most beautiful people we have known are those who have known defeat, known suffering, known struggle, known loss, and have found their way out of the depths. These persons have an appreciation, a sensitivity, and an understanding of life that fills them with compassion, gentleness, and a deep loving concern. Beautiful people do not just happen.

Will The Adversity You Face Give You Motivation to Do Good?

First Peter 4:12-19 says:

> Dear friends, don't be bewildered or surprised when you go through the fiery trials ahead, for this is no strange, unusual thing that is going to happen to you. Instead, be really glad—because these trials will make you partners with Christ in his suffering, and afterwards you will have the wonderful joy of sharing his glory in that coming day when it will be displayed.

> Be happy if you are cursed and insulted for being a Christian, for when that happens the Spirit of God will come upon you with great glory. Don't let me hear of your suffering for murdering or stealing or making trouble or being a busybody and prying into other people's affairs. But it is no shame to suffer for being a Christian. Praise God for the privilege of being in Christ's family and being called by his wonderful name! For the time has come for judgment, and it must begin first among God's own children. And if even we who are Christians must be judged, what terrible fate awaits those who have never believed in the Lord? If the righteous are barely saved, what chance will the godless have? So if you are suffering according to God's will, keep on doing what is right and trust yourself to the God who made you, for he will never fail you.

Mark Victor Hansen refers to adversity when he says,

> Don't wait until everything is just right. It will never be perfect. There will always be challenges, obstacles and less than perfect conditions. So what? Get started now. With each step you take, you will grow stronger and stronger, more and more skilled, more and more self-confident, and more and more successful.

Will the Adversity You Face Produce Happiness?

James 1:12 says:

> Happy is the man who doesn't give in and do wrong when he is tempted, for afterwards he will get as his reward the crown of life that God has promised those who love him.

I'm reminded of the story of the man who was griping about the problems, trials, and adversity in his life. He moaned and groaned that the burden he had to bear was too difficult.

"I would sure like to get rid of this very heavy cross," he said one day.

Zap! All of a sudden he was ushered into heaven and found himself standing before St. Peter. "What am I doing here?" he asked. "Did I die?"

"No," said St. Peter. "I just heard you complaining about your cross, and I thought I would help you out. Come with me to the Warehouse of Crosses. We'll see if we can find you a new one."

The man followed St. Peter. Inside the large warehouse were big crosses and little crosses. Wooden crosses and glass crosses. There were some heavy metal crosses and crosses of all colors, shapes, and forms. There was even a large cross on wheels making it easier to move.

St. Peter said, "You can go anywhere in the warehouse you like and select the cross of your choice."

"Wow! That's a great plan," said the man.

He began walking through the warehouse looking at all the crosses. It took him hours before he finally found one to his liking. It was a very small, light, aluminum cross. He took it back to St. Peter for approval.

"A great choice," said St. Peter. "That's the very same cross you've been carrying."

If all misfortunes were laid in one common heap whence everyone must take an equal portion, most people would be contented to take their own and depart.

SOCRATES

> *Acceptance of one's life has nothing to do with
> resignation; it does not mean running away from
> the struggle. On the contrary, it means accepting it
> as it comes, with all the handicaps of heredity, of
> suffering, of psychological complexes and injustices.*
>
> PAUL TOURNIER

Will the Adversity You Face Help You to Comfort Others?

Second Corinthians 1:3-7 says:

> What a wonderful God we have—he is the Father of our
> Lord Jesus Christ, the source of every mercy, and the one
> who so wonderfully comforts and strengthens us in our
> hardships and trials. And why does he do this? So that when
> others are troubled, needing our sympathy and encourage-
> ment, we can pass on to them this same help and comfort
> God has given us. You can be sure that the more we undergo
> sufferings for Christ, the more he will shower us with his
> comfort and encouragement. We are in deep trouble for
> bringing you God's comfort and salvation. But in our trou-
> ble God has comforted us—and this, too, to help you: to
> show you from our personal experience how God will ten-
> derly comfort you when you undergo these same sufferings.
> He will give you the strength to endure.

Jerry Bridges reminds us:

> One thing we may be sure of, however: for the believer all
> pain has meaning; all adversity is profitable. There is no
> question that adversity is difficult. It usually takes us by sur-
> prise and seems to strike where we are most vulnerable. To
> us it often appears completely senseless and irrational, but
> to God none of it is either senseless or irrational. He has a
> purpose in every pain He brings or allows in our lives. We
> can be sure that in some way He intends it for our profit
> and His glory.

Adversity is just one of the hurdles in life

Dear God,

Wow! I can tell I've been focusing on my difficulties, disappointments, and discontents. It's been a bad day, my horn is stuck, and I feel like the motorcycles behind me are gaining speed. I'm beginning to think I've brought some of my troubles on myself. I think I need to give up, stop resisting, and submit to the lessons I need to learn. I need Your help in this test tube of fiery trials. I need You to help me mature and grow. I need You to help me accept the situation I'm in and pick up my cross—one that is quite small compared to those some people carry—and to move on in life. I'm a little tired of running around in circles. Please give me the energy I need to leap over the hurdles of adversity I'm facing.

Amen.

Attitude Is a Choice...So Pick a Good One.

11

ATTITUDE AND FORGIVENESS

*Forgiveness is the key that unlocks the door of resentment
and the handcuffs of hatred. It is a power that breaks the
chains of bitterness and the shackles of selfishness.*

CORRIE TEN BOOM

I just can't get that tune out of my head." Have you ever heard a song or lyrics you keep remembering...over and over in your mind? The song continually interferes with your thoughts—and it becomes very difficult for you to think about anything else.

This is a type of *rumination*: a combination of concentration, pondering, and repeating a thought over and over. It's a form of mentally "chewing on" various comments, problems, or situations in your life.

When cows eat grass or hay, they swallow the food, later vomit it up into their mouths, chew it some more, and then swallow it again. This process is called "chewing the cud."

When someone hurts you or disappoints any expectations you have for them, negative feelings can arise. Like the cow chewing the cud, we can vomit up negative thoughts, hurtful comments others have made, or situations that have been mentally harmful for us. We keep remembering the event or comment over and over again.

The difference between cows and humans is significant when it comes to rumination. When cows chew their cud, they feel peace and contentment. Relaxed cows chew their cud; cows under stress do *not* chew their cuds. Humans, however, are usually under various degrees of stress when they chew over their problems and difficulties. Ruminating for humans can cause high blood pressure, anxiety, anger, disappointment, resentment, weakened immune systems, loss of sleep, labored breathing, ulcers, muscle tension, sweating, trembling and shaking, digestive issues, and a host of other physical ailments.

You may ask, "What's the best and fastest way to break the ruminating process of negative thinking and feeling? How can I choose a good attitude?" There's a simple answer, but it's not an *easy* answer. A great portion of the rumination in our lives revolves around someone who has said or done something to hurt us. After thinking about what happened for a while, we come to the conclusion that what that person or persons did or said to us was not fair. We become hurt, then angry, then resentful. Then we develop a grudge, and then we want some type of vindication or revenge. Welcome to Hurtsville; a lot of people live here.

Now back to the simple answer: *We need to forgive them.*

"Wait a minute," you say. "What they did was not right or true. It was not fair. They wanted to hurt me. They need to pay for what they did."

Slow down. Take a deep breath. Forgiveness is not a benefit for your enemy. Forgiveness is a benefit for you. With forgiveness, you break the rumination process. You pop the balloon of hatred and revenge. You release yourself from the prison of negative thinking. You can then spend your emotional energy in getting your act together. You can plan your future. You can have some peace of mind for a change. Doesn't that sound better than what you've been doing that hasn't worked? Has all your brooding over the past changed anything?

Dale Carnegie makes an interesting comment when he says, "When we hate our enemies, we are giving them power over us: power over our sleep, our appetites, our blood pressure, our health, and our happiness. Our enemies would dance with joy if only they knew how they were worrying us, lacerating us, and getting even with us! Our hate is not hurting them at all, but our hate is turning our days and nights into a hellish turmoil."

> *When you forgive, you in no way change the*
> *past—but you sure do change the future.*
>
> BERNARD MELTZER

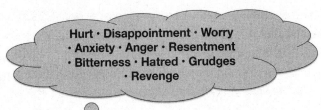

Forgiveness Can Set You Free

Why Is It So Difficult to Forgive?

- We're sinful, selfish, and self-centered.

- We have a strong need and desire for control. We don't like it when we are no longer in control.

- We prefer guarantees over uncertainty. We don't like feeling helpless in situations.

- We desire superiority over others. Feeling inferior does not feel good.

- We have our own views of fairness, and when treated unfairly, we desire vindication, revenge, or retaliation.

- We have human thoughts and emotions, and we get hurt easily.

> *In forgiveness, the offended party suffers the pain of hurt and loss and the offender goes free. This is a dirty deal…right!*
>
> R.E. PHILLIPS

Who Needs to Be Forgiven?

- Our parents need to be forgiven for things they did wrong—especially when we consider that we want our children to forgive us for what we did wrong or are doing wrong right now.

- We need to forgive ourselves. It's amazing that we don't even live up to our own expectations.

- Our mates or family members need to be forgiven. Has there ever been a perfect home, where no one got angry or hostile, or where no one ever said or did the wrong things?

- We must forgive those in power who did not exercise authority well. This could include teachers, police, bosses, church leaders, and especially politicians. They really need it!

- We need to forgive everyone else not on this list.

What Are the Biggest Reasons for Forgiving?

First, forgiveness is not a feeling; forgiveness is a command. Forgiveness is mandatory. It's an act of the will. It's a choice we must make. We have been instructed to forgive.

> Get rid of all bitterness, rage, anger, harsh words, and slander, as well as all types of evil behavior. Instead, be kind to each other, tenderhearted, forgiving one another, just as God through Christ has forgiven you (Ephesians 4:31-32 NLT).

> Do not judge others, and you will not be judged. Do not condemn others, or it will come back against you. Forgive others, and you will be forgiven (Luke 6:37 NLT).

> Make allowance for each other's faults, and forgive anyone who offends you. Remember, the Lord forgave you, so you must forgive others (Colossians 3:13 NLT).

If another believer sins against you, go privately and point out the offense. If the other person listens and confesses it, you have won that person back. But if you are unsuccessful, take one or two others with you and go back again, so that everything you say may be confirmed by two or three witnesses (Matthew 18:15-16 NLT).

Parable of the Unforgiving Debtor

Peter came to him and asked, "Lord, how often should I forgive someone who sins against me? Seven times?"

"No, not seven times," Jesus replied, "but seventy times seven!

"Therefore, the Kingdom of Heaven can be compared to a king who decided to bring his accounts up to date with servants who had borrowed money from him. In the process, one of his debtors was brought in who owed him millions of dollars. He couldn't pay, so his master ordered that he be sold—along with his wife, his children, and everything he owned—to pay the debt.

"But the man fell down before his master and begged him, 'Please, be patient with me, and I will pay it all.' Then his master was filled with pity for him, and he released him and forgave his debt.

"But when the man left the king, he went to a fellow servant who owed him a few thousand dollars. He grabbed him by the throat and demanded instant payment.

"His fellow servant fell down before him and begged for a little more time. 'Be patient with me, and I will pay it,' he pleaded. But his creditor wouldn't wait. He had the man arrested and put in prison until the debt could be paid in full.

"When some of the other servants saw this, they were very upset. They went to the king and told him everything that had happened. Then the king called in the man he had forgiven and said, 'You evil servant! I forgave you that tremendous debt because you pleaded with me. Shouldn't you have mercy on your fellow servant, just as I had mercy on you?' Then the angry king sent the man to prison to be tortured until he had paid his entire debt.

"That's what my heavenly Father will do to you if you refuse to forgive your brothers and sisters from your heart" (Matthew 18:21-35 NLT).

> *Not forgiving is like drinking rat poison*
> *and then waiting for the rat to die.*
>
> ANNE LAMOTT

Second, forgiveness provides the groundwork for healing, reconciliation, and restoration of relationships. It creates emotional peace.

You may ask: "Does that mean if I forgive someone we'll automatically have reconciliation between us and a restoration of the relationship?"

No, it doesn't. Forgiveness is a one-way street. One person obeys and forgives another. Reconciliation, on the other hand, is a two-way street. Both parties must have the desire to restore their relationship for reconciliation to work. Unfortunately, your forgiving someone else does not guarantee they'll want to forgive you, let alone reconcile with you. It may be a cold day in the hot place before they will ever give up their anger toward you. This is the really hard side of forgiveness. You will experience peace in your heart because of your obedience to forgive...but peace between the two of you may never be possible. Remember, God forgives, but not all want to be reconciled with Him. You will experience in a small way what God experiences in a large way.

> *You will never forgive anyone more than*
> *God has already forgiven you.*
>
> MAX LUCADO

Third, we're reminded that we are not to foster bitterness or resentment, nor are we owed vindication or revenge for the wrongs done to us. Our job is not to go around collecting "hurt stamps" to put in a "grudge book" as proof of how life has been so unfair to us. Hello, does that bring joy to your heart?

> Bless those who persecute you. Don't curse them; pray that God will bless them. Be happy with those who are happy, and weep with those who weep. Live in harmony with each other. Don't be too proud to enjoy the company of ordinary people. And don't think you know it all!
>
> Never pay back evil with more evil. Do things in such a way that everyone can see you are honorable. Do all that you can to live in peace with everyone.
>
> Dear friends, never take revenge. Leave that to the righteous anger of God. For the Scriptures say, "I will take revenge; I will pay them back," says the LORD. Instead, "If your enemies are hungry, feed them. If they are thirsty, give them something to drink. In doing this, you will heap burning coals of shame on their heads." Don't let evil conquer you, but conquer evil by doing good (Romans 12:14-21 NLT).

*We all agree that forgiveness is a beautiful
idea until we have to practice it.*

C.S. LEWIS

Practical Help for Attitude Change in the Area of Forgiveness

When the hornet of memory flies into your mind, learn how to take out its sting. Practice steps for finding the off button of negative thinking.

- *Respond quickly* when bad attitude thoughts raise their ugly head.
- *Acknowledge* their presence.
- *Question* your unrealistic thoughts; do not just accept them as fact.

- *Distract yourself* by taking a mind detour.
  - *Pray.*
  - *Read your Bible.*
  - *Talk to someone.*
  - *Do a task you have been putting off.*
  - *Watch a movie.*
  - *Read a book.*
  - *Listen to music.*
  - *Get some counsel.*
  - *Exercise or go for a walk.*

- *Determine* what set off the negative thinking. Identify the triggers and then eliminate them.

- *Follow* the steps of Matthew 18:15; talk with the individual with whom you have a problem.
  - *Acknowledge and accept your anger.*
  - *State your hurt as objectively as possible. Do not overstate or exaggerate the issue.*
  - *Acknowledge the other person's feelings.*
  - *Listen, receive, and accept their apology if it is offered. Do not attempt to get even.*
  - *Try to gain an understanding between you. This does not mean you will achieve total agreement, but understanding each other's feelings goes a long way in the clarification of issues.*

> *Forgiveness is a sign that the person who has wronged you means more to you than the wrong they have dealt.*
>
> **BEN GREENHALGH**

Forgiveness Exercise

1. Think of an event that has been difficult for you. What sort of forgiveness is needed?

2. Who is the individual you need to forgive?

3. List reasons why you have not been able to forgive.

4. What do you think Jesus would like you to do in this particular situation?

5. Do you need to ask anyone to forgive you for your attitude and actions? What do you think Jesus would like you to say to this person?

6. Make a list of people you should pray for.

Dear God,

To forgive others is a big order. I do not know how You did it. It is so difficult to forgive someone who has hurt me. I think I want to, but the memory of the event comes back time and again to haunt me. Sometimes I live it over and over. Help me to drive the hornet of memory away. Please take away his big stinger. Please draw out the poison of bitterness and resentment. Teach me how to think about positive things and let go of the past. I know I need to go to some people and ask for forgiveness. I have hurt them. Please give me the courage to do this. Give me the right words to say to help heal their pain. Thank You for loving me enough to die for me and forgive my sins. Help me to exhibit the same godly and forgiving spirit as You did for me.

Amen.

Attitude Is a Choice...So Pick a Good One.

12

ATTITUDE AND GRATITUDE

Gratitude, like faith, is a muscle. The more you use it, the stronger it grows, and the more power you have to use it on your behalf. If you do not practice gratefulness, its benefaction will go unnoticed, and your capacity to draw on its gifts will be diminished. To be grateful is to find blessings in everything. This is the most powerful attitude to adopt, for there are blessings in everything.

ALAN COHEN

I f you think you have problems, read *The Bricklayers Story* by Gerard Hoffnug:

> When I got to the building I found that the hurricane had knocked some bricks off the top. So I rigged up a beam with a pulley at the top of the building and hoisted up a couple of barrels full of bricks. When I had fixed the building, there was a lot of bricks left over. I hoisted the barrel back up again and secured the line at the bottom, and then went up and filled the barrel with the extra bricks. Then I went to the bottom and cast off the line. Unfortunately the barrel of bricks was heavier than I was, and before I knew what was happening the barrel started down, jerking me off the ground.
>
> I decided to hang on, and halfway up I met the barrel coming down and received a severe blow on the shoulder.
>
> I then continued to the top, banging my head against the beam and getting my finger jammed in the pulley. When the barrel hit the ground it bursted its bottom, allowing all the bricks to spill out.
>
> I was now heavier than the barrel and so started down again

at high speed. Halfway down, I met the barrel coming up and received severe injuries to my shins. When I hit the ground I landed on the bricks, getting several painful cuts from the sharp edges. At this point I must have lost my presence of mind because I let go the line. The barrel came down, giving me another heavy blow on the head and putting me in the hospital. I respectfully request sick leave.

> *Of all the "attitudes" we can acquire, surely the*
> *attitude of gratitude is the most important*
> *and by far the most life-changing.*
>
> ### ZIG ZIGLAR

Every man and woman that walks the face of planet earth faces problems and trials of varying degrees. No one can or will escape problems, but your attitude about problems is what counts. Paul the apostle reminds us in 1 Thessalonians 5:18: "Be thankful in all circumstances, for this is God's will for you who belong to Christ Jesus" (NLT).

Whether you have a cracked fingernail, a snag in your sweater, broken eyeglasses, or a pain in your body, nothing that happens to you isn't first checked out and filtered by the heavenly Father.

Remember what Paul says in James 1:2-4: "Dear brothers, is your life full of difficulties and temptations? Then be happy, for when the way is rough, your patience has a chance to grow. So let it grow, and don't try to squirm out of your problems. For when your patience is finally in full bloom, then you will be ready for anything, strong in character, full and complete."

*Without dark clouds in our lives we would never
know the joy of sunshine. We can become callous
and unteachable if we do not learn from pain.*

BILLY GRAHAM

The Attitude of Gratitude in the Midst of Problems, Trials, and Trouble

A Life of Trials—Job

The book of Job is dedicated to Job's life and his many overwhelming trials. It can be summed up with Job's own words: "The Lord gave me everything I had, and they were his to take away. Blessed be the name of the Lord" (Job 1:21).

Triple Trouble—Jehoshaphat

In 2 Chronicles 20, King Jehoshaphat encountered trouble when three armies decided to attack him at the same time. Consider developing some of Jehoshaphat's attitudes, which can be applied to the difficulties you might be facing.

Verse 3—He was "badly shaken" by the news and sought help from the Lord. As Psalm 46:1 reminds us, "God is our refuge and strength, a tested help in times of trouble."

Verse 4—The entire nation joined him in prayer for deliverance.

Verse 7—They claimed a promise from God of help.

Verse 12—They admitted that they were helpless before their big problem: "We don't know what to do, but we are looking to you."

Principle #1—The Battle Is Not Yours but God's

Verses 14-16—Encouraging words come from God through Jahaziel: "The Lord says, 'Don't be afraid! Don't be paralyzed by this mighty army! For the battle is not yours, but God's!"

*We know that all that happens to us is working for our
good if we love God and are fitting into his plans.*

ROMANS 8:28

Principle #2—You Play a Part

Verses 16-17—"Tomorrow, go down and attack them! You will find them coming up the slopes of Ziz at the end of the valley that opens into the wilderness of Jeruel. But you will not need to fight! Take your places; stand quietly and see the incredible rescue operation God will perform for you, O people of Judah and Jerusalem! Don't be afraid or discouraged! Go out there tomorrow, for the Lord is with you!"

The Bible is full of stories where the men and women of God had to participate in their difficulties. They exercised their human energy to the fullest and trusted God to do what they could not do. They faced their problems and believed in the God of miracles. Paul the apostle talks the roles we play when he says, "For God is at work within you, helping you want to obey him, and then helping you do what he wants" (Philippians 2:13).

Principle #3—Thank God for the Victory Before the Battle

Verses 18-19—"Then King Jehoshaphat fell to the ground with his face to the earth, and all the people of Judah and the people of Jerusalem did the same, worshiping the Lord. Then the Levites of the Kohath clan and the Korah clan stood to praise the Lord God of Israel with songs of praise that rang out strong and clear."

Principle #4—Put the Singers in Front

Verse 20-21—"Early the next morning the army of Judah went out into the wilderness of Tekoa. On the way Jehoshaphat stopped and called them to attention…'Believe in the Lord your God and you shall have success! Believe his prophets and everything will be all right!' After consultation with the leaders of the people, he determined that there should be a choir leading the march, clothed in sanctified garments and singing the song 'His Loving-Kindness Is Forever' as they walked along praising and thanking the Lord!"

Jehoshaphat's plan was to send a group of singers (a choir) out in front of the army to praise God. How would you like to be in a singing group marching to battle ahead of the army? Can you imagine what the enemy thought as they saw a choir marching toward them? We know the singers were afraid because the Bible records that Jehoshaphat "appointed" singers. There were no volunteers!

The word *singers* translated literally means praisers. In other words, we need to put the *praisers* ahead of the battle.

One phrase is key to verse 22: "at the moment." God did not do anything until the praisers began to sing. "At the moment" they began, God performed a miracle. Similarly, at the point when our faith becomes action, God meets us with a miracle answer. You may not get any volunteers from your emotions at a time of stress. You may have to *appoint* some singers in your life as an act of faith and with the strength of will.

God will meet you in your faith. Will you join the choir? Will you step out and praise the Lord in the face of your problem…before you even see His answer for you?

> *I will praise the Lord no matter what happens. I will constantly speak of his glories and grace. I will boast of all his kindness to me. Let all who are discouraged take heart. Let us praise the Lord together and exalt his name. For I cried to him and he answered me! He freed me from all my fears.*
>
> PSALM 34:1-4

A Big Problem—Paul and Silas

In Acts 16, Paul and Silas were faced with an angry mob that dragged them before the judges at the marketplace. They were accused of a trumped-up charge: teaching the people of the city to do things that were against the Roman laws. The mob was especially angry that Paul and Silas had cast a demon out of a fortune teller who had earned much money for her masters.

Verses 22-24 explain the big problem they faced: A mob was quickly formed against Paul and Silas, and the judges ordered them stripped and beaten with wooden whips. Again and again the rods slashed down across their bared backs; and afterwards they were thrown into prison. The jailer was threatened with death if they escaped, so he took no chances, but put them into the inner dungeon and clamped their feet into stocks.

Paul and Silas put the singers out in front. They praised God in the middle of their problem even though they had no idea how He could help them. In verses 25-27, Scripture tells us what Paul and Silas were doing before God answered their prayers:

> Around midnight, as Paul and Silas were praying and sing-ing hymns to the Lord—and the other prisoners were listen-ing—suddenly there was a great earthquake; the prison was shaken to its foundations, all the doors flew open—and the chains of every prisoner fell off! The jailer wakened to see the prison doors wide open, and assuming the prisoners had escaped, he drew his sword to kill himself.

It is important to develop an attitude of gratitude regardless of your situation, problems, or trials.

All the Days of My Life—A Song of Praise

The Lord is my shepherd—
all the days of my life
I shall not want—
all the days of my life
He maketh me to lie down
in green pastures—
all the days of my life
He leadeth me beside the still waters—
all the days of my life
He restoreth my soul—
all the days of my life
He leadeth me in the paths
of righteousness for His name's sake—
all the days of my life
Yea, though I walk through the valley
of the shadow of death—
all the days of my life
I will fear no evil—
all the days of my life
For thou art with me—

all the days of my life
Thy rod and thy staff they comfort me—
all the days of my life
Thou prepares a table before me
In the presence of mine enemies—
all the days of my life
Thou anointest my head with oil—
all the days of my life
My cup runneth over—
all the days of my life
Surely goodness and mercy shall follow me—
all the days of my life
And I will dwell in the house
of the Lord forever—
all the days of my life.

PSALM 23, ADAPTED BY BOB PHILLIPS

Reflect upon your present blessings—of which
every man has many—not on your past
misfortunes, of which all men have some.

CHARLES DICKENS

First and foremost, our expression of gratitude should be directed toward our Creator and the blessings He has showered upon us.

With Jesus' help we will continually offer our sacrifice of
praise to God by telling others of the glory of his name.

HEBREWS 13:15

Along with that, you also need to express gratitude to your family of origin, friends, teachers, fellow workers, church leaders, neighbors, and everyone you come in contact with. Showing gratitude helps you to develop deeper relationships and brings about personal happiness for you and for others. Gratitude encourages patience and improves an optimistic spirit.

THE INFLUENCE OF GRATITUDE

Gratitude is a virtue.

Gratitude is well received.

Gratitude is a state of being.

Gratitude is a matter of habit.

Gratitude is saying thank you.

Gratitude is showing appreciation.

Gratitude rejoices in all situations.

Gratitude comes from a generous spirit.

Gratitude is the opposite of entitlement.

Gratitude recognizes the value of others.

Gratitude takes the focus off yourself.

Gratitude gives credit where credit is due.

Gratitude comes from a sense of well-being.

Gratitude enriches the lives of other people.

Gratitude loves to give recognition to others.

Gratitude helps others grow in their happiness.

Gratitude can turn a common meal into a feast.

Gratitude gives you an opportunity to trust God.

Gratitude comes from a positive thinking process.

Gratitude creates positive interpersonal relationships.

Gratitude is recognizing the hand of God in everything.

Gratitude from within should demonstrate its actions without.

Gratitude encourages others to pass on gratitude to more people.

An Experimental Investigation of Gratitude and Subjective Well-Being in Daily life

Robert A. Emmons   Michael E. McCullough
University of California, Davis   University of Miami

People who displayed gratitude:

- had fewer physical symptoms and felt better as a whole

- had lower levels of unpleasant emotions

- had better sleep duration and lower levels of stress and depression

- were more optimistic and made more progress toward their goals

- were more alert, more enthusiastic, more determined, more attentive, and had more energy

- had a sense of feeling connected with others

- helped others with personal problems, offering emotional support and encouragement

*Gratitude is the single most important ingredient
to living a successful and fulfilled life.*

JACK CANFIELD

──── Gratitude Exercise ────

Do you have people in your life who have helped and encouraged you? Maybe they're your own parents or siblings. It might have been your grandparents. It could have been a special teacher. It might be a trusted friend or a mentor who spent time with you. It could even be someone you have not personally met, but you heard them speak or they wrote something that changed the course of your life. Are you grateful for their influence and support?

1. Take a few moments and make a list of these special and important people in your life.

2. Decide to show gratitude to them. You can visit them personally, you could call them, or you could write them a note or letter expressing your appreciation for their influence and impact.

3. Consider writing a handwritten note. Not an e-mail or text message. "Why?" you may ask. Because letter writing is a lost art. Let me ask you a question. Do you have somewhere in your files any written letters or notes of encouragement that you've kept? Most of us do. I have a number of them. The reason we keep them is because of how those words impacted us and made us feel. Why not do the same for the people who have helped you grow and mature? Show your thankfulness in writing for what they have done.

4. Plan an entire letter-writing week. Or you might extend it into two weeks or even a letter-writing month. You will be surprised what this time will do for your own attitude about life.

You might even want to create a gratitude journal. Begin listing all the things you are grateful for. If possible, attempt to write something to be thankful for each day and keep it going for a whole year. That would give you at least 365 things to be grateful for. Why not give it a try?

> *You simply will not be the same person two months from now after consciously giving thanks each day for the abundance that exists in your life. And you will have set in motion an ancient spiritual law: the more you have and are grateful for, the more will be given you.*
>
> SARAH BAN BREATHNACH

> *You say grace before meals. All right. But I say grace before the concert and the opera, and grace before the play and pantomime, and grace before I open a book, and grace before sketching, painting, swimming, fencing, boxing, walking, playing, dancing and grace before I dip the pen in the ink.*
>
> G.K. CHESTERTON

Here are some thoughts to get you started. Begin your own list and see how many you can name.

——— A Few Things to Be Thankful For ———

Ability to Breathe
Ability to Read
Ability to See
Ability to Write
Adventures
Air-Conditioning
A Listening Ear
Art
Babies
Blue Sky
Books
Cell Phones
Challenges
Colors
Comfortable
    Shoes
Computers
Cozy Evenings
Deep
    Conversations
Education
Eyes
Faith
Fall Leaves
Family Traditions
Favorite Armchair
First Kiss
Forgiveness
Freedom

Fresh Snow
Friends
Fun
Getting Good
    News
Gift of Life
Good Hair Days
Good Memories
Good Sleep
Grandparents
Great Movies
Great Quotes
Grocery Stores
Guidance
Health
Hobbies
Holidays
Home-Cooked
    Meals
Honesty
Hope
Hot Showers
Laughing
Legs and Feet
Love
Loyalty
Medicine
Mentors

Money in the
    Bank
Music
New Beginnings
Oceans
Parents
Peace
Pets
Positive People
Power Naps
Purpose in Life
Rain
Road Trips
Roof over Your
    Head
Scenic Drives
Seasons
Smiles
Success
Sunsets
Sunshine
Transportation
Trees
Warm Hugs
Weekends
Wildflowers
Work
Your Bed

Dear God,

Thank You for reminding me that I'm not the only person who has encountered problems in life. When I think of all the trials You faced in sending Your Son to undergo suffering for me, I'm put to shame. Please give me the patience to face my difficulties with a positive attitude. Thank You for the lessons of praise and gratitude from Job, Jehoshaphat, and Paul and Silas. Please help me to put singers out in front of my worries and concerns. Please bring to my mind the individuals I need to express gratitude to this next month. Help me to write words of thanks and encouragement to those who have supported me. Most of all, thank You for dying on the cross for my sins, that I might enjoy Your presence throughout eternity. And thank You for all the daily provisions You make available to me. I am truly fortunate and blessed by Your grace and mercy.

Amen.

Attitude Is a Choice...So Pick a Good One.

13

ATTITUDE AND FAITH

*Faith is this extraordinary principle which links man to God; faith
is this thing that keeps a man from hell and puts him in heaven; it is
the connection between this world and the world to come; faith is this
mystic, astounding thing that can take a man dead in trespasses and
sins and make him live as a new being, a new man in Christ Jesus.*

MARTYN LLOYD-JONES

Have you ever gone on a cave tour? If so, have you traveled far enough into the cave to have an eerie feeling and wonder: *What would happen if I get trapped inside and cannot get out?* On most cave tours, there's a point when the guide turns off every light and leaves you in total darkness. The guide will then ask you to hold up your hand and look at your fingers. Try as you may, you cannot see your hand. All you encounter is overwhelming blackness. Close your eyes for a moment and imagine what it would be like to never see light again. How would you feel?

When it comes to God's attributes of grace and mercy, they cannot be fully appreciated until one comes to view the darkness of the heart. Most of us don't like to view ourselves as depraved and without good qualities. We may acknowledge that we're not perfect, but we're certainly not as bad as Hitler, terrorists, or others who have committed great atrocities. What is your attitude about this thing called sin?

On the other hand, what is the standard for goodness? What do you measure your thoughts, words, and actions against? Is there a comparison sheet for good and bad desires, motives, and goals? Often we justify and compare ourselves to others, hoping our goodness will somehow outweigh our badness. When it comes to Judgment Day, many hope God will see more positives than negatives and give them permission to enter heaven.

If a scale that measured badness and goodness existed, where would you place yourself on that scale? If ten is perfection, are you somewhere in the middle?

——— Badness—1 2 3 4 5 6 7 8 9 10—Goodness ———

God has a different evaluation scale. He doesn't compare one human being to another human being to determine their badness or goodness. He compares human beings to Himself. God doesn't have any badness in His nature, being, or essence. God is holy, righteous, and good. Now, the question is: How do you think you match up? If God is a ten, where are you on the scale?

As God holds up the light of His holiness to the darkness of our hearts, what does He see? We think we have some goodness when compared to others, but how does God view our goodness? Let's look at what the Bible says.

> "Who can say, 'I have kept my heart pure; I am clean and without sin'?" (Proverbs 20:9 NIV).

> "If we claim to be without sin, we deceive ourselves and the truth is not in us" (1 John 1:8 NIV).

> "For all have sinned and fall short of the glory of God" (Romans 3:23 NIV).

> "They have all turned aside, together they are corrupt; there is no one who does good, not even one" (Psalm 14:3 NASB).

> "All of us have become like one who is unclean, and all our righteous acts are like filthy rags; we all shrivel up like a leaf,

and like the wind our sins sweep us away. No one calls on your name or strives to lay hold of you; for you have hidden your face from us and have given us over to our sins" (Isaiah 64:6-7 NIV).

"What shall we conclude then? Do we have any advantage? Not at all! For we have already made the charge that Jews and Gentiles alike are all under the power of sin. As it is written: 'There is no one righteous, not even one; there is no one who understands; there is no one who seeks God. All have turned away, they have together become worthless; there is no one who does good, not even one'" (Romans 3:9-12 NIV).

Wow! That's pretty straightforward! If God views us as dead in our transgressions and sins, then what is needed? We need life! We need light to destroy the darkness that separates us from the light in God. We need grace and mercy from the wrath and punishment of the Almighty. We are lost in the darkness, wandering in our blindness without any escape from the bottomless cave of separation. The cave of separation is known as total spiritual depravity. We have no ability in ourselves to become righteous and holy as God is. That's the bad news.

Now for the good news! You can experience a complete revision of your sinful attitude and nature—and it's a free gift if you will accept it.

"For the wages of sin is death, but the gift of God is eternal life in Christ Jesus our Lord" (Romans 6:23 NIV).

"That as sin hath reigned unto death, even so might grace reign through righteousness unto eternal life by Jesus Christ our Lord" (Romans 5:21 KJV).

More good news! God, in His supreme loving-kindness, chose to shower you with His wonderful grace and His undeserved mercy. Grace is the bestowing of God's favor and forgiveness on undeserving humans.

It cannot be purchased with money, fame, or power. Grace is an unwarranted gift, free-flowing from the heart of a loving God.

> For God so loved the world that he gave his one and only Son, that whoever believes in him shall not perish but have eternal life. For God did not send his Son into the world to condemn the world, but to save the world through him. Whoever believes in him is not condemned, but whoever does not believe stands condemned already because they have not believed in the name of God's one and only Son (John 3:16-18 NIV).

> Consequently, just as one trespass resulted in condemnation for all people, so also one righteousness act resulted in justification and life for all people. For just as through the disobedience of the one man the many were made sinners, so also through the obedience of the one man the many will be made righteous. The law was brought in so that the trespass might increase. But where sin increased, grace increased all the more, so that, just as sin reigned in death, so also grace might reign through righteousness to bring eternal life through Jesus Christ our Lord (Romans 5:18-21 NIV).

Jesus, Full of Grace—
John 1:14

The Gift of Grace—
Roman 5:15

Law and Grace—
John 1:17-18

Abundant Grace—
Romans 5:17

Saved by Grace—
Acts 15:11

Chosen by Grace—
Romans 11:5-6

Justified by Grace—
Romans 3:22-25

The Riches of Grace—
Ephesians 1:7-9

Grace and Peace—
Romans 5:1-3

Grace Encourages —
2 Thessalonians 2:16-17

Grace and Purpose—
2 Timothy 1:8-10

Grace for Needs—
Hebrews 4:16

Grace That Teaches—
Titus 2:11-14

Steadfast in Grace—
1 Peter 5:10-11

Take a moment and ponder this question: Why did God choose to display His grace to us? We're all so undeserving of His great love. The very thought should break us and humble us, as we contemplate our good fortune.

I'm also aware that it's possible that a reader of these words may not yet have received the free gift of grace in Christ. If that's the case, you can do it right now. You might ask, "How is that done?" You may accept the gift by following Paul's words in Romans 10:8-13.

> But what does it say? "The word is near you; it is in your mouth and in your heart," that is, the message concerning faith that we proclaim: If you declare with your mouth, "Jesus is Lord," and believe in your heart that God raised him from the dead, you will be saved. For it is with your heart that you believe and are justified, and it is with your mouth that you profess your faith and are saved. As Scripture says, "Anyone who believes in him will never be put to shame." For there is no difference between Jew and Gentile—the same Lord is Lord of all and richly blesses all who call on him, for, "Everyone who calls on the name of the Lord will be saved" (NIV).

Mercy involves God's forbearance in putting off a trial and well-deserved punishment. His mercy is a grand display of His compassion to an offender, as well as a demonstration of divine forgiveness for an offense. It's an extreme exhibition of kindness arising from God's goodness and love.

Sovereign Mercy

"And the LORD said, 'I will cause all my goodness to pass in front of you, and I will proclaim my name, the LORD, in your presence. I will have mercy on whom I will have mercy, and I will have compassion on whom I will have compassion'" (Exodus 33:19 NIV).

Entrance Made Possible by Mercy

"But as for me, I will come into your Temple protected by your mercy and your love; I will worship you with deepest awe" (Psalm 5:7).

Saved by Mercy

"When the kindness and love of God our Savior appeared, he saved us, not because of righteous things we had done, but because of his mercy. He saved us through the washing of rebirth and renewal by the Holy Spirit, whom he poured out on us generously through Jesus Christ our Savior, so that, having been justified by his grace, we might become heirs having the hope of eternal life" (Titus 3:4-7 NIV).

Great Mercy—
1 Chronicles 21:13

Mercy That Forgives —
Psalm 25:6-7

The Love of Mercy—
Micah 6:8

The Task of Mercy—
Matthew 5:7

The Mystery of Mercy—
Romans 11:32-36

The Working Out of Mercy—
Romans 12:1-2

The Source of Mercy—
Ephesians 2:4-5

The Triumph of Mercy—
James 2:12-13

The Vastness of Mercy—
James 5:11

The Result of Mercy—
1 Peter 1:3-5

Wonderful Grace of Jesus

Wonderful grace of Jesus,
Greater than all my sin;
How shall my tongue describe it,
Where shall its praise begin?
Taking away my burden,
Setting my spirit free;
For the wonderful grace of Jesus reaches me.

Wonderful the matchless grace of Jesus,
Deeper than the mighty rolling sea;
Wonderful grace, all sufficient for me, for even me.
Broader than the scope of my transgressions,
Greater far than all my sin and shame,
O magnify the precious name of Jesus.
Praise His name!

Wonderful grace of Jesus,
Reaching to all the lost,
By it I have been pardoned,
Saved to the uttermost,
Chains have been torn asunder,
Giving me liberty;
For the wonderful grace of Jesus reaches me.

Wonderful grace of Jesus,
Reaching the most defiled,
By its transforming power,
Making him God's dear child,
Purchasing peace and heaven,
For all eternity;
And the wonderful grace of Jesus reaches me.

HALDOR LILLENAS

Dear God,

When it comes to my sinfulness, I'm aware of the darkness of my attitudes, thoughts, and actions. I know I don't match up to Your standard of holiness. The thought of You loving me in spite of my behavior is overwhelming. Thank You for Your grace, mercy, and loving-kindness. Thank You for sending Your son to die in my place and take the penalty for my sins. I want to confess Jesus Christ as my Savior and Lord. I believe He was raised from the dead that I might have eternal life. I want to experience everything You have in store for me. I need an extreme makeover for my life—a reworking of my attitude of selfishness. I need Your strength to love others and show grace and mercy to them. Help me to begin with my own family. Make me a person who thinks of others and their needs. Come into my life and transform me. Please lead me out of the cave of darkness and into Your presence. I need the light.

Amen.

Attitude Is a Choice...So Pick a Good One.

14

ATTITUDE AND CAREER

Twenty years from now you will be more disappointed by the things you didn't do than by the ones you did do. So throw off the bowlines. Sail away from the safe harbor. Catch the trade winds in your sails. Explore. Dream. Discover.

H. JACKSON BROWN JR.

How long do you plan to stay in your job? In an article written by Chris Kolmar, he suggests that the average person changes their job about 12 different times in their lifetime. Many of these individuals spend five years or less in every job. Other surveys suggest that the average person changes careers between five and seven times.

Gallup poll indicates that Only 13% of full-time workers are passionately and deeply engaged and connected with their job. The poll goes on to state that 63% of those workers are not engaged. These individuals are unhappy, checked out, and have little energy for their work. What is striking is that 24% are actively disengaged and hate their jobs.[4]

Maybe you have met some of these mildly or actively disengaged employees. They often come across as either uninterested or intolerant of customers and visitors. You feel like you're imposing on them by asking a question or requesting help. They're often seen as lazy or bored, or they demonstrate great ability for disappearing when real work has to be done. The bathroom calls them often. They can be seen surfing the Internet, answering text messages, and spending time at the water cooler. What they lack in work ethic they make up for in anger and impatience. They are highly skilled in gossiping, sowing discord, and creating drama. They also have the unique ability to change their behavior like a chameleon if doing so is in their best interest.

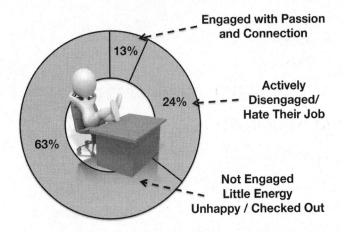

Where do you see yourself on the spectrum? Are you a passionately engaged employee, a moderately engaged employee, or an actively disengaged employee who defiantly hates your job?

> *If you don't like something, change it. If you*
> *can't change it, change your attitude.*
>
> MAYA ANGELOU

Maybe you're thinking, *I'm not an angry or lazy employee, but I am a little bored and unhappy with my present job. I want to have a positive attitude about my career and my future employment.*

If so, good. That's an excellent place to start. What would you like to do? What type of work excites you? Basically two types of jobs exist: the kind you can *tolerate*—one that puts food on table and pays the bills—and the kind you *love*, which also puts food on the table and pays the bills. The choice is yours.

I'm aware it's not always an easy task to find work you truly love. The Gallup poll indicates that most workers have not found it. So join the club.

What follows is the *Finding My Way Inventory*. It was created to help you narrow your field of interest and focus on what you would consider satisfying, exciting, and fulfilling work. One of the ways it helps you is to eliminate the things you do not want to do. Take some time and work your way through the inventory, marking the boxes and answering the questions asked. Just as attitude is a choice, many of your dreams and aspirations will also require some choices. Enjoy.

———— Finding My Way Inventory ————

Please be as honest as possible with your answers.

CHOOSE ONE OPTION — Make a Choice:

General Questions

Where do you want to live?

☐ East Coast ☐ West Coast ☐ Middle America ☐ North
☐ Middle States ☐ South ☐ Other

Do you want to live outside the United States? If so, where would you like to live?

You prefer: ☐ Overcast weather ☐ Sunshine

You want to live: ☐ Close to relatives ☐ Far from relatives
☐ Somewhere between

You would like to stay near your:
☐ Hometown ☐ It doesn't matter

You would rather live in the: ☐ City ☐ Country

Work-Related Thoughts and Questions

Do you want to work in a: ☐ Warm climate ☐ Cold climate

Do you prefer to:
☐ Work with people ☐ Work on tasks and projects

Do you want to: ☐ Work outside ☐ Work inside

You'd like to: ☐ Work by yourself ☐ Work with others

Your preferred work pace is: ☐ Slow ☐ Fast

You prefer to: ☐ Lead others ☐ Follow others

You see yourself as: ☐ A self-starter ☐ Motivated by others

You prefer to: ☐ Make final decisions ☐ Have others decide

You need: ☐ Lots of structure ☐ Lots of freedom

You need to be physically active in a job: ☐ Yes ☐ No

Energetically, you are: ☐ High energy ☐ Low energy

With regard to organization, you are:
☐ Organized ☐ Disorganized

With regard to punctuality, you are:
☐ Usually on time ☐ Usually late

At work you like to dress: ☐ Casually ☐ It doesn't matter

You would prefer to be known for your:
☐ Carefulness ☐ Capabilities

You would prefer to be appreciated for your:
☐ Contributions ☐ Cleverness

You need leadership that: ☐ Gives suggestions ☐ Allows freedom
☐ Provides direction ☐ Provides inspiration

You tend to be irritated by: ☐ Missed deadlines
☐ Illogical tasks ☐ Pressure ☐ Rules

You see yourself as a: ☐ Very hard worker ☐ Strong worker
☐ Average worker ☐ Relaxed worker

Your attitude toward work is: ☐ Very positive ☐ Somewhat
positive ☐ Somewhat negative ☐ Very negative

With regard to authority:
☐ You struggle with it ☐ You don't struggle with it

You like working on:
☐ Short-term projects ☐ Long-term Projects

With regard to education:
☐ You want or need more ☐ You're satisfied with your level

With regard to change:
☐ You view change as an opportunity or challenge
☐ You view change as stressful and something to be controlled

You measure progress by: ☐ Activity ☐ Results
☐ Approval ☐ Applause

What charges your emotional batteries and gives you the most energy at work?

☐ Being with and enjoying people
☐ Planning and completing tasks and goals

❖

Place a ranking number following each item:
1—being first 2—being second—etc.

You prefer a work situation with:

Private workspace, systems to improve efficiency, excellence awards.   _____

Increased responsibility, leadership roles, merit raises, fringe benefits.   _____

Sincere praise and appreciation, personal gifts, acts of kindness.   _____

Flexible scheduling, parties, public praise, recognition for creativity.   _____

You get the most job satisfaction from:

Creating ideas and concepts for the first time.   _____

Creating ideas and concepts and transforming them into actions and practical results.   _____

Taking other people's ideas and projects and developing, improving, and polishing them.   _____

Developing ideas and projects along with administrating tasks.   _____

Managing tasks, systems, facts, and the many details of an organization.   _____

You tend to focus on:

Details and perfection.   _____

Results and goal orientation.   _____

Consensus and unity.   _____

Excitement and energy.   _____

❖

You would like:

☐ To be self-employed   ☐ To work for a corporation

☐ To work in a small business   ☐ To work for a nonprofit

☐ To work in a church   ☐ To work for a para-church organization

☐ Other _____

List your skills and abilities:

_____

_____

_____

To you, money and salary are:

_____

_____

_____

If money were no object, you would like to:

_____

_____

_____

The most important thing about work is:

_____

_____

_____

Do you need a job that has social impact? If so, why?

What energizes you about your work?

❖

Relational Questions

You see yourself as: ☐ Reserved ☐ Outgoing

You tend to be: ☐ Less confrontational
☐ More confrontational

You tend to be: ☐ A good listener ☐ A poor listener

You see yourself as: ☐ More strict ☐ More permissive

You see yourself as: ☐ Liberal ☐ Conservative

With regard to small talk: ☐ You like it
☐ You shy away from it

With regard to emotions: ☐ You guard them
☐ You share them

People would say you're: ☐ Easy to get to know
☐ Hard to get to know

With regard to decisions: ☐ You will not pressure people
for them ☐ You tend to pressure people for them

When involved in conflict, you: ☐ Withdraw—become
less assertive ☐ Dominate—become over assertive
☐ Give in—seek peace and reduce conflict
☐ Attack—share strong emotions

❖

Personal Questions

You see yourself as: ☐ Introverted ☐ Extroverted

You see yourself as: ☐ Preoccupied ☐ Carefree

You see yourself as: ☐ Patient ☐ Impatient

You see yourself as: ☐ Serious ☐ Playful

Your driving emotion under stress is: ☐ Fear ☐ Anger

With regard to your opinions, you: ☐ Reserve them
☐ Share them

With regard to risk taking, you: ☐ Avoid it ☐ Don't mind it

With regard to time, you're: ☐ Disciplined
☐ Less disciplined

You tend to be motivated to: ☐ Save face ☐ Save time
☐ Save effort ☐ Save relationships

What would you like to go to school to learn?

_____

_____

You tend to daydream about:

_____

_____

What makes you laugh?

_____

_____

What keeps you up at night?

_____

_____

Your biggest drain of joy comes from:

Your biggest fear is:

Your biggest frustration is:

Your usual response to criticism is:

What hurts you most is:

Your biggest struggle is:

To you, life is:

Your biggest question is:

You would like help:

_____

_____

You tend to worry about:

_____

_____

You tend to be depressed by:

_____

_____

You would like to change the habit of:

_____

_____

You would measure success by:

_____

_____

The biggest obstacle holding you back is:

_____

_____

What do you want to be remembered for?

_____

_____

What would you do if you knew you could not fail?

_____

_____

Other Questions and Concerns:

_____

_____

❖

Spiritual Questions

The person who had the biggest influence in your life was:

_____

_____

**Your first contact with any kind of spiritual warmth
or influence was:**

_____

_____

To you, God is:

_____

_____

You think church is:

_____

_____

How would you characterize your relationship with God?

_____

Are you carrying a burden you need to trust God with?

When it comes to displaying the fruits of the Spirit, you struggle most with:

☐ Love, joy, and kindness—*Analytical Social Style*

☐ Love, patience, and gentleness—*Driving Social Style*

☐ Love, peace, and endurance—*Amiable Social Style*

☐ Love, self-control, and faithfulness—*Expressive Social Style*

Other Questions or Concerns:

Information on Various Careers

You may find the Internet very beneficial in your career search. Use your favorite search engine (such as Google or Mozilla) to search "career choices" or "list of careers." I also suggest searching for "career tests" to help you further explore your interests and options. Most of these resources are free. Super cool.

Mike Rowe, the *Dirty Jobs* guy, expressed his thoughts about work when he said:

> Happiness does not come from a job. It comes from knowing what you truly value, and behaving in a way that's consistent with those beliefs. Many people today resent the suggestion that they're in charge of the way they feel. But trust me, those

people are mistaken. That was a big lesson…and I learned it several hundred times before it stuck. What you do, who you're with, and how you feel about the world around you, is completely up to you.[5]

> *What is the recipe for successful achievement? Choose*
> *a career you love. Give it the best there is in you. Seize*
> *your opportunities. And be a member of the team.*
>
> BENJAMIN FRANKLIN FAIRLESS

26 Questions to Ask Yourself Before Making Major Decisions

Not every question in this list will be helpful in every situation. This is simply a checklist for guidance—a resource to keep you from overlooking important considerations before carrying out major decisions.

1. Are there any alternatives that should be considered before you decide?

2. Are there any questions that still need to be answered before you decide?

3. Are you dealing with the root of a problem or the symptom of a problem?

4. Are you tired? Do you need some rest before you make this decision?

5. As you pray about this decision, do you have a sense of confidence and peace?

6. Do you feel comfortable about the best timing for your decision?

7. Do you have confidence in your decision?

8. Does the Bible have anything to say about the situation you're facing?

9. Does this decision affect your values, standards, character, or goals?

10. Have you talked with others who have made similar decisions?

11. If you were forced to make a decision in the next two minutes, what would it be?

12. In one sentence, what is the issue or decision you're facing right now?

13. Should you consider: Who? What? When? Where? Why? How? How much?

14. What additional facts would help you make your decision?

15. What decision do you think your family and friends would suggest for you?

16. What is driving your need to make a change at this time?

17. What is the emotional driving force for the decision you are considering?

18. What will be the costs and the benefits of your decision?

19. What would happen if you did not carry out this decision?

20. What would the ideal solution for your situation be? The best-case scenario?

21. Will this decision help or hinder you from reaching your ultimate goals?

22. Will your decision be in line with your key strengths and skills?

23. Will your decision make a difference one year, five years, or ten years from now?

24. Would it be good to think for at least 24 more hours before making this decision?

25. Would it be helpful to break your decision down into smaller sub-decisions?

26. Would it be helpful to seek advice and outside counsel?

*Trust in the LORD with all your heart and lean not on your own understanding;
in all your ways submit to him, and he will make your paths straight.*

PROVERBS 3:5-6 NIV

Show me your ways, LORD, teach me your paths. Guide me in your truth and teach me, for you are God my Savior, and my hope is in you all day long.

PSALM 25:4-5 NIV

For this God is our God for ever and ever; he will be our guide even to the end.

PSALM 48:14 NIV

Dear God,

I don't want to spend my time in a dead-end job. I want a job that not only satisfies my physical, mental, and emotional growth but also brings me fulfillment as I make contributions to society. Regardless of the career, I pray I may be a strong witness for You in whatever I do. In the process of discovering the right job for me, I pray You will give me great wisdom. Help me to find counselors or people in a particular field of interest who can give me guidance. Please give me patience during this search, as well as a spirit of openness and flexibility. I can hardly wait to see where You will lead me. Thank You in advance, and may I learn to trust You in everything I do.

Amen.

Attitude Is a Choice...So Pick a Good One.

15

ATTITUDE, CHANGE, AND TRANSITION

It isn't the changes that do you in, it's the transitions. Change is not the same as transition. Change is situational: the new site, the new boss, the new team roles, the new policy. Transition is the psychological process people go through to come to terms with the new situation. Change is external, transition is internal.

WILLIAM BRIDGES

"Clarissa, you've been a new mother for a month now. How is it going?" asked Rita.

"I love my baby with all my heart, but he sure has changed our lifestyle. Bill and I aren't getting the sleep we used to, and breastfeeding is an entirely new experience. Don't get me wrong; we're thrilled that little Bill Jr. is here…but I'm so tired."

So what else is new? I think we all understand deep down that the entire world is in a state of change. Some changes are good, and some changes are not so good. And when it comes to individual circumstances and experiences, everyone has their own unique story.

The Greek philosopher Heraclitus suggested that nothing remains the same even if there's a sense of unity. Take, for example, the flame of a candle. When lit, all candles are unified in that they all have a flame. Yet each flame is in constant movement and change, so no two flames are ever the same in their movement. Heraclitus went on to say: "You cannot step twice into the same river." The river might appear to be the same because the water flows by ceaselessly. However, the moment you step into the water, it's gone.

You may be thinking, *Why is he talking about a Greek philosopher?*

It's because all of mankind has a similar unity of experiences, yet each experience is different for every person. We all have joys and sorrows, high times and low times, health and illness.

So what?

So we all have to make peace with the fact that life is filled with changes.

Life Is a Flow of Constant Change—Nothing Remains the Same

- Birth
- Infancy
- Adolescence
- Early Adulthood
- Marriage

- Parenthood
- Empty Nest
- Retirement
- Widowhood
- Death

There Is Winter—Spring—Summer—Fall

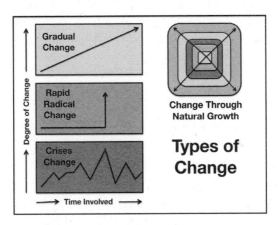

Some changes we face are *temporary*. For example, the average person moves about 11 times in their lifetime. The average American drives between 8 and 12 cars in their lifetime. Researchers do not agree but suggest that the average woman changes her hairstyle between 104 and 150 times in her lifetime. These are all temporary changes that one chooses to make. Temporary changes are forced upon us sometimes, such as being

laid off. Perhaps a drunk driver destroys our car and causes us unnecessary expenses, or someone accidently spills grape juice on our brand-
new white carpet. Although these events may be disruptive, expensive, or
emotionally frustrating, they are not forever experiences. They are more
short-term changes or interruptions.

To improve your attitude amid these types of situations:

- take a deep breath

- look at these changes objectively

- endure the unnecessary expenses

- try to make adjustments so the inconveniences may not
  happen again

- let go of your anger or frustration

Remember, life is too short to spend your time and energy on these
types of issues.

> *There is certain relief in change, even though it be
> from bad to worse! As I have often found in travelling
> in a stagecoach, that it is often a comfort to shift
> one's position and be bruised in a new place.*
>
> WASHINGTON IRVING

On occasion, changes will come into your life that could be considered *permanent*. These types of long-term changes are life-altering. Several years ago I accidently cut off part of my left thumb with a crosscut
saw. That event has left me with constant, low-grade nerve pain in the
remaining part of my thumb. The loss makes it very difficult to button
small buttons on the collars of shirts, and I struggle to pick up small
items. This is not a temporary change. It's definitely permanent.

Other permanent changes in life could include illnesses like heart
disease, cancer, or diabetes. We all know someone who has gone through
a divorce. You may be one of them. Divorce is not a temporary change.
You're either divorced or you're not. There's no in-between. The death of
a family member or friend is an ultimate, permanent change. When it

comes to such life-altering events, you have to learn to make peace with them and accept what is beyond your control.

God grant me the serenity
To accept the things I cannot change;
Courage to change the things I can;
And wisdom to know the difference.
Living one day at a time;
Enjoying one moment at a time;
Accepting hardships as the pathway to peace;
Taking, as He did, this sinful world
As it is, not as I would have it;
Trusting that He will make all things right
If I surrender to His Will;
So that I may be reasonably happy in this life
And supremely happy with Him
Forever and ever in the next.
Amen.

REINHOLD NIEBUHR

Anatole France addresses the concept of permanent change when he suggests: "All changes, even the most longed for, have their melancholy; for what we leave behind us is a part of ourselves; we must die to one life before we can enter another." On the same subject, Joseph Campbell writes: "We must let go of the life we have planned, so as to accept the one that is waiting for us."

Transition

The uncomfortable place between letting go of the safe and familiar past and moving toward an unknown or uncertain future. It is terrifying and exhilarating all at the same time.

*At the threshold of every transition in our lives the devil sends
a spirit of fear. Therefore be strong and very courageous!*

CHRISTINE CAINE

Change or transition usually involves more than one event or circumstance happening at the same time. Juggling many events and emotions is not an easy task. Let's take divorce, for example. Before a divorce becomes legal, it brings with it a weighted past. This past involves a number of complicated issues, such as:

Anger	Fears	Hurt
Arguments	Finances	School
Children	Friends	Unfaithfulness
Family	Health	Work

Divorce then leads to a transition time between any future relationships or second marriage. This is a painful time when both parties must let go of the past—including the hope of reconciliation, their hurt and anger, and their desire for revenge. This transition time is one of fear and uncertainty as to what the future holds. *What's going to happen to the children? Will I be able to retain the same friends? Will I have to move? Will I make it financially? Will it affect my future vocation? Will I ever get married again? What will people think of me?*

Similar questions arise when you lose a job, move to another town, encounter health problems, or face the death of a loved one. Yet you

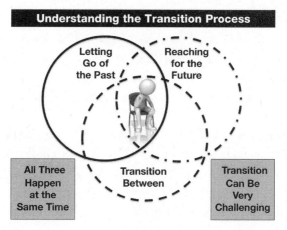

must let go of a past you cannot change. You cannot avoid a transition time. And you *will* struggle as to what the future holds. This is a common path.

After a transition period awaits the new world of the future…the idea of which is a little scary, intimidating, and unsettling. But here's the kicker: The process of letting go of the past, experiencing transition, and facing an uncertain future are not phases you go through one at a time. *They all happen at once.* Now, it becomes a little more understandable why change, which is more about external events, and transition, which is more about your internal responses to change, are so complex and overwhelming. Unfortunately, no class you can take will teach you how to deal with change and transition. In school you usually study a certain topic and then take a test to see what you remember; but in life, experience is the test itself—and *then* you learn the lesson. *Yikes!*

Nature teaches us that in the fall, leaves change color, die, and drop from the trees. In a similar way, changes often cause bright and colorful dreams to fade, grow dark, fall to the ground, and die. Some dreams fade slowly and others quite quickly.

> When one door closes, another opens; but we often
> look so long and so regretfully upon the closed door
> that we do not see the one which has opened for us.
>
> AUTHOR UNKNOWN

In the Old Testament, Job is a classic example of someone who endured short-term temporary changes and long-term permanent changes. In the first chapter of Job, he *temporarily* loses his oxen, donkeys, sheep, camels, and house. He also *permanently* loses his farmhands when the Sabeans raid, his herdsmen in a fire, his servants when the Chaldeans attack, and his sons and daughters in a terrible windstorm. *Double yikes!*

Job then faces a tremendous health crisis. His wife does not support him, and three friends criticize him. Young men make fun of him, associates turn against him, and he loses his reputation. For days he's filled with depression, sees no escape from his trials and troubles, and thinks death would be better than life for him. *Triple yikes!*

During the fall season of Job's life, most of his dreams fade and die. He then moves into an emotional winter—a season when he can find no answers for his questions about the disasters in his life. He endures this winter transition period for 37 chapters.

In chapters 38-42, Job's transition period changes to springtime. He begins to gain insight that God has never left him. Job realizes that God is in control and is not caught off guard by Job's trials, difficulties, loneliness, and hurt. Not until the last eight verses of chapter 42 does Job move out of his transition and into his new summertime of peace and happiness.

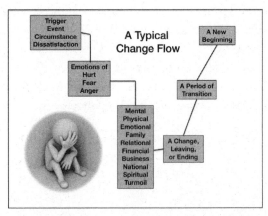

Remember, after an emotional change event, we often go through a transition period of confusion, disorientation, and frustration before we become peaceful, readjusted, and comfortable with a new future. There is no detour or way to skip the transition period. You *will* have to go through it. You can, however, go through transitions with a positive attitude and trust in God, or you can choose to experience transitions with a negative attitude. The choice is yours. In which season of life do you find yourself?

Keep Rowing

After Jesus fed the 5,000, He went up into the mountains alone (Matthew 14:21-34). His disciples then got into a boat and began rowing across the Sea of Galilee toward Gennesaret. It was evening when they entered the boat. They had rowed a few miles when the sea grew rough and a powerful, contrary wind began to blow. Soon they were pounded and tossed about as the storm increased. Great storms were common on the Sea of Galilee, and it was made even worse because of the darkness. With the absence of light, the disciples were uncertain of the direction they were rowing.

Have you ever been rowing on the sea of life, going in a particular direction, when dark circumstances rose up against you—followed by a great storm of anxiety and depression? Have you felt the pounding of emotional waves that seemed to engulf you and toss your thoughts all around? Have you felt like you were going to drown? Have you experienced hope departing and the feeling you're at your wit's end?

So did the disciples. I'm sure they wondered where Jesus was in their time of need. Didn't He care they were afraid? Didn't He understand the danger they were in?

How did the disciples respond to their difficult, distasteful, and disappointing circumstance? They kept rowing, and rowing, and rowing in the midst of the storm. They didn't give up in despair.

——— That's the Message: Keep On Rowing ———

Amid the watery transition the disciples faced, Jesus walked on the water and got into the boat with them. Everything gets calm when Jesus is in your boat. Often all you see are the dark clouds of trouble and the storms of adversity. You're not aware that God is behind the scenes working out His plan for your life. But why does He wait? Is it not because when He does come, His hand of relief will be all the more evident? The brilliance of His help will come at just the right time, when you're at the point of losing all hope.

> The ropes of death entangled me; floods of destruction swept over me. The grave wrapped its ropes around me; death laid a trap in my path. But in my distress I cried out to the LORD; yes, I prayed to my God for help. He heard me from his sanctuary; my cry to him reached his ears. Then the earth quaked and trembled. The foundations of the mountains shook; they quaked because of his anger. Smoke poured from his nostrils; fierce flames leaped from his mouth. Glowing coals blazed forth from him. He opened the heavens and came

down; dark storm clouds were beneath his feet. Mounted on a mighty angelic being, he flew, soaring on the wings of the wind. He shrouded himself in darkness, veiling his approach with dark rain clouds. Thick clouds shielded the brightness around him and rained down hail and burning coals. The LORD thundered from heaven; the voice of the Most High resounded amid the hail and burning coals. He shot his arrows and scattered his enemies; great bolts of lightning flashed, and they were confused. Then at your command, O LORD, at the blast of your breath, the bottom of the sea could be seen, and the foundations of the earth were laid bare. He reached down from heaven and rescued me; he drew me out of deep waters (Psalm 18:4-16 NLT).

Security

There were twelve of the apostles
On that bitter, storm-tossed sea.
But only one was able there
To challenge you and me.
Peter walked upon the water
Til he touched the Savior's hand.
But where were the eleven
Other ones in Jesus' band?
Where was James, and where was Thomas,
Watching Peter's stumbling feet?
They were grasping their security
On a fragile, storm-stressed seat.
There came a day that gallant ship
Lay sinking hopelessly.
Then everyone cried, "Save us, Lord!"
And cried it lustily.
Yes, all of us must meet Him,
In the ship, or on the sea.
So why not walk the water,
Where the wind blows free?

HERMON PETTIT

So Can You!

Jay Adams shares the following story:

> I once drove through the "Garden of the Gods" outside Colorado Springs. In this beautiful natural wonder you can see rocks balanced on a pinpoint and vividly colored scenery on all sides. As you drive along slowly, viewing the marvels about you, suddenly you are confronted with a problem: directly ahead of you looms a wall of sheer rock, and the road on which you are traveling disappears into what seems be a crack so narrow that it looks as though you'd have a hard time driving a VW car through it. Looking around for a place in which to turn and go back your eye falls on a small white sign. It reads:

—Narrows—

Yes You Can
A Million Others Have

> And what do you know—a minute and a half later, a million and one have done it.[6]

You're not alone. Millions of other people are going through the same things you're facing. The way has been narrow for them also. They have learned how to face their fears, hurts, and temptations—and overcome their anxiety and depression. How? They learned to trust and rely on God to come to their need. So can you. Keep rowing.

> *For He [God] Himself has said, I will not in any*
> *way fail you nor give you up nor leave you without*
> *support. [I will] not, [I will] not, [I will] not in any*
> *degree leave you helpless nor forsake nor let [you]*
> *down (relax My hold on you)! [Assuredly not!]*
>
> HEBREWS 13:5 AMPC

Dear God,

Help me to understand and be alert to changes that are situational and external—as well as transition, which is more psychological and internal. Help me to accept that change is happening in all areas of my life. When temporary changes come, help me avoid blowing them out of proportion. Teach me to accept permanent changes and make peace with things I cannot change...and grant me the ability to know the difference. Give me the courage to let go of past experiences and hurts. Create in me a positive vision for the future. Help me to keep on rowing through rough water, as the disciples and Job did. Thank You for reminding me that I'm not the only one who is going through tough times—that just as millions of others have done, may I trust You also for meeting my daily needs. Thank You for reminding me that You will never leave me or forsake me no matter the situation. Thank You for that tremendous promise.

Amen.

Attitude Is a Choice...So Pick a Good One.

16

EVALUATING NEGATIVE ATTITUDES

One employee who is always negative will eventually wear down the positive attitudes of those around him, and your entire team will end up behaving in a negative manner.

TERRANCE SEMBER

How do you deal with negative attitudes in the workplace? You as a leader may be called upon to deal with a troublesome employee who's in need of correction, discipline, or possibly firing. How do you document the behavior that needs to be corrected?

Being late to work, stealing from the employer, or fighting on the job are easy-to-document situations. What's difficult is disciplining employees who have *poor attitudes.*

How do you document a negative attitude? It's so subjective. For this reason, the following form was designed to help clarify and describe someone's attitude in terms of their words, tones of voice, and nonverbal behaviors. This form can be of use in helping to document conflict that occurs as a result of what is commonly called "attitude."

Employees with negative attitudes often do not see themselves as problematic. When confronted, they might easily reply, "What do you mean when you say I've got a negative, hostile, or bad attitude?" What would you say in response? How can you help the employee become aware of their behavior?

This is a subjective evaluation, but attitude is just as real as any other aspect of an employee's performance. The evaluation focuses primarily on how fellow workers or supervisors feel about, and whether they can work in harmony with, the individual.

One way to help a negative individual to gain insight is to describe their behavior in terms of:

(1) the *words* they use

(2) their *tone of voice* while speaking to others

(3) the *nonverbal behaviors* that accompany their interactions with fellow employees, customers, or the general public

Use the chart that follows as a guideline. For each of the boxes checked, provide a real-life example to help the individual understand the effects of their actions on others.

For example:

☒ RUDENESS Yesterday in our meeting you made this comment to Carla: "Why don't you quit your whining, put on your big girl pants, and just do the job?"

☒ SIGHING I have noticed you sighing in disagreement when you are asked to do something. It seems to indicate—or it comes across as though—you're upset, annoyed, or feel put-upon. Is that what you are trying to convey?

☒ GESTURES I noticed that after your supervisor asked you to do something and he turned his back, you gave him the finger and stuck out your tongue. Does that help you to understand why I may be concerned about your negative attitude? You are not using words to communicate your feelings, but your nonverbal behavior speaks volumes.

The world is full of people who complain, who look for the negative in life, and who are constantly pulling each other down. The world is full of people who think only of themselves and try to make the rest of the world as miserable as they are.

JESSICA JONES

No one forces a person to be negative, and no one forces anyone to be positive. The choice is up to an individual and that person alone.

BYRON PULSIFER

Attitude in Performing the Actual Work and the Corresponding Interpersonal Relationships Involved

Attitude is a consistent state of mind or feeling that, over a period of time, manifests itself through words, tones of voice, and nonverbal behaviors.

Look at the three categories & check all that apply & illustrate attitude problems.

Types of Words	Tone of Voice	Nonverbal Behavior
☐ Put-down humor	☐ Talking down	☐ Little eye contact
☐ Pessimistic	☐ Mimicking	☐ Walking away
☐ Angry	☐ Whining	☐ Ignoring
☐ Hostile	☐ Argumentative	☐ Hand and finger signs
☐ Rude	☐ Defensive	☐ Silent, angry stare
☐ Sarcastic	☐ Accusing	☐ Gritting of teeth
☐ Lying	☐ Yelling	☐ Making faces
☐ Bitter	☐ Attacking	☐ Throwing things
☐ Negative	☐ Grumpy	☐ Folding arms
☐ Gossip	☐ Grouchy	☐ Pouting
☐ Slander	☐ Impatient	☐ Tears
☐ Divisive	☐ Angry, cross	☐ Yawning
☐ Critical	☐ Testy, catty	☐ Raising eyebrows
☐ Irritated	☐ Sighs, grunts	☐ Frowning
☐ Spiteful	☐ Exasperated	☐ Angry looks

Dear God,

Dealing with negative attitudes has been given to me as a responsibility. Please give me the wisdom to deal with this difficult situation. Help me to not jump the gun without getting all the facts first. Help me to listen to all sides of the issue. Help me to be fair, kind, and firm. Help me to remember that the goal is to help change negative behavior into positive behavior…if possible. Help me to stick to the key issues and not be derailed or sidetracked with things that are unimportant. Give me courage to deal with conflict as You would. Thank You in advance for the help You will give me.

Amen.

Attitude Is a Choice…So Pick a Good One.

ATTITUDE TREASURE CHEST

*The way to happiness: Keep your heart free from hate,
your mind from worry. Live simply, expect little, give
much. Scatter sunshine, forget self, think of others. Try
this for a week and you will be surprised.*

NORMAN VINCENT PEALE

*There is little difference in people, but that little difference makes a
big difference. The little difference is attitude. The big difference is
whether it is positive or negative.*

W. CLEMENT STONE

Zamboni Thinking

Where I used to work, we maintained an
ice-skating rink. Visitors enjoyed skating
around the rink as music played in the
background. On occasion we also hosted
hockey games for the more active individuals. Whether people were skating to music or
involved in intense activity on the ice, they all

had one thing in common: The blades on the skates they wore created
marks, crevices, and divots in the ice. During the hockey games, sometimes chunks of ice were taken out of the ice when collisions occurred
between the players.

It doesn't take a great deal of time before the ice becomes a little
rough to skate on. Grooves in the ice can sometimes catch a blade and
cause the skater to stumble or even fall. Take my word for it: Falling
down on ice and hitting your head is not a pleasant experience at all.

To help make the surface of the ice smooth, we used a machine called
a Zamboni. The Zamboni has a blade that scrapes the ice and two augers
that collect the snow, which is later discarded. Following the blade is a

spray unit that fills the cracks, grooves, and crevices in the ice with a fine mist. A blanket assists in spreading the water evenly. Before the invention of the Zamboni, resurfacing a skating rink used to take several people three hours or more. Now the job takes about ten minutes.

You are like a Zamboni when it comes to your attitude. You can choose to wipe away the cracks of negative thinking. You can fill the grooves of hurt with kindness, compassion, and forgiveness. You can even learn to fill the deep holes of disappointment in broken relationships with the water of God's Word. Just as the augers pick up snow scraped from the ice and discard it, you can learn to discard anxiety, worry, anger, resentment, guilt, and vengeful thoughts.

The Zamboni's tank is filled with water to spray over the rough and ragged ice. Likewise, before you attempt to level out the cracks of your bad attitudes, make sure your mental and emotional tank is filled with the water of God's Word. In the back of this book, you will find Bible verses on over 250 different topics. They will help you learn how to smooth out the difficulties of life.

Making Decisions

Many people have a hard time making decisions. They don't want to make the wrong decision, and the fear of doing so makes them put off or prolong coming to any conclusion on a matter. As a result, they may say things like, "I don't want to make a decision before I get all the facts."

The truth is, if you wait until you get all the facts, it will no longer be a decision. It will be a conclusion. Decisions are made without all the facts. That's why they're called *decisions.*

When it comes to issues and decisions, it's important to determine if they will have short-term or long-term effects—in other words, if they are temporary or permanent types of decisions.

For example: Let's say you need to decide about your next job for employment. Of course, you'll get as many facts and details as you can to help you make a decision. You will look at the pros and the cons, talk to people who may be acquainted with the company, and try to gather as much information as you can to help in a decision. But do you really have all the *facts?*

- Do you fully understand the personalities of the people you would be working with? *Those are important facts.*

- Do you really know and understand what type of boss you'll be working for? *That's an important fact.*

- You may have received a job description, but do you fully understand the unwritten and unspoken expectations involved? *Unspoken expectations are really important facts.*

- All organizations have a culture, set of values, and sometimes what we call politics. Are you aware of all those facts before you make a decision? *These are important facts, but we don't always find them out before we make a decision.*

When it comes to timing, we're sometimes forced to make decisions before we have time to gather all the facts. Also, when it comes to emergencies, we may have to make life-and-death decisions without the benefit of all the facts or sufficient information.

If someone is shooting at us, we can't stop and say, "Let's take a few moments and attempt to discover what led that young man into a life of crime. Did he come from a troubled family? Did his parents get a divorce? Did he get into arguments with schoolmates?" Maybe it would be good to make a quick decision to run for your life.

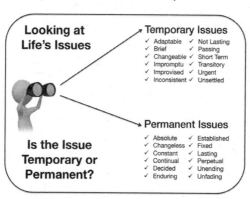

Now, for the clincher: When we decide to marry someone, do we have all the facts before we say yes? I don't think so. We make the best decisions we can without all of the known facts. Many decisions are made without all the facts. That's why they're called decisions instead of conclusions.

It is good to consider the various components of decision-making—which is simply choosing between various courses of action:

- investigating the facts and gathering information
- exploring and creating alternatives or options
- using reasoning and logic
- determining the benefits or losses
- considering the effect on other people
- understanding your fears and concerns
- evaluating your plan with good counsel
- designing a possible backup plan
- trusting your intuition and instincts
- making the decision

In *View from the Cockpit* by Archie B. Lawson, he shares this story about former president Ronald Reagan,

> This account contributed to how he became a great decision maker. An aunt had taken him to a cobbler to have a pair of shoes made for him. The shoemaker asked young Ronald Reagan, "Do you want a square toe or a round toe?"
>
> Reagan hemmed and hawed. So the cobbler said, "Come back in a day or two and let me know what you want."
>
> A few days later the shoemaker saw Reagan on the street and asked what he had decided about the shoes. "I still haven't made up my mind," he answered. "Very well," said the cobbler.
>
> When Reagan received the shoes, he was shocked to see that one shoe had a square toe and the other a round toe.

"Looking at those shoes every day taught me a lesson," said Reagan years later. "If you don't make your own decisions, somebody else will make them for you!"[7]

The reason we want other people to help us with decisions is so when the decision goes wrong we can turn back to our counsel and say, "You dirty dog! It's your fault. You talked me into it." It's time for you to have a positive attitude and make your own decisions. It's time to put on your big boy or big girl pants and decide.

> *Decision is the spark that ignites action. Until a decision is made, nothing happens. Decision is the courageous facing of issues, knowing that if they are not faced, problems will remain forever unanswered.*
>
> WILFERD PETERSON

The Worst-Case Scenario

To accept an issue, problem, or difficulty is the first step in overcoming the consequences of misfortune. True peace of mind comes from an attitude of submission to the situation—from contemplating the worst possible outcome and working forward from there. When we accept the worst, we have nothing more to lose. Everything else is a gain from there. Problems are things you work on; facts of life are things you accept and learn to make peace with.

Let's say you learn from your doctor that you have cancer. What is the worst possible outcome? You could die. Once you accept that worst case, any improvement from there is a blessing to be received.

Mother Goose, the great psychologist, taught us a positive attitude principle early in life with the following lines:

> For every ailment under the sun,
> There is a remedy, or there is none;
> If there be one, try to find it;
> If there be none, never mind it.

*The difficulty we have in accepting responsibility
for our behavior lies in the desire to avoid the
pain of the consequences of that behavior.*

M. SCOTT PECK

*Another way to be prepared is to think negatively. Yes, I'm a
great optimist. But when trying to make a decision, I often
think of the worst case scenario. I call it "The Eaten by Wolves
Factor." If I do something, what's the most terrible thing that
could happen? Would I be eaten by wolves? One thing that
makes it possible to be an optimist is if you have a contingency
plan for when all hell breaks loose. There are a lot of things I
don't worry about because I have a plan in place if they do.*

RANDY PAUSCH

You're Not the Boss of Me!

If you have young children in your home, you might hear the expression, "You're not the boss of me!" Siblings especially say this when one child tells the other what to do or how to act.

Has the same thought ever come across your mind? "You're not the boss of me!" "I disagree with you!" "That's a stupid idea!" "Hang it in your ear; I'm not going to do it!" You might have used other words, but you get the idea.

When we're placed in a disagreeable situation, a spirit of rebellion often rises inside us. We don't want to comply with the request or demand. We don't want to submit, give in, or bow down to them. We want to do our own thing. Have you ever felt that way?

When you see a sign that says "Wet Paint: Do Not Touch," what's your first desire? When you see a sign that says, "Don't Walk on the Grass," what do you want to do most? When I was a kid, my older brother would hold me down, twist my arm behind my back, and say, "Give up!" What do you think my response was?

It was, "Never!" Even through the tears and pain, I never gave in. Even if he had come close to breaking my arm, I would not have given in to him. Have you ever been there? Well, as you can see, I have.

The attitude of determination and endurance—even in the face of pain—can be beneficial under certain circumstances. However, when a determined attitude becomes hostile and rebellious, negative consequences can occur.

When it comes to people who have legitimate authority over you—parents, teachers, bosses, police, etc.—how do you respond? Do you submit, or do you become noncompliant?

The story of Samuel the prophet and King Saul appears in 1 Samuel 15. Samuel comes to Saul with a message from God regarding battle plans Saul was to carry out. King Saul does not verbally say no to Samuel and the instruction from God; but he goes ahead and does his own thing, contrary to God's command. In essence he says, "You're not the boss of me!" But because he refuses to submit to legitimate authority, Saul must face the consequences.

Later, when Samuel confronts King Saul about his rebelliousness and disobedience, he says,

> "When you didn't think much of yourself, God made you king of Israel. And he sent you on an errand and told you, 'Go and completely destroy the sinners, the Amalekites, until they are all dead.' Then why didn't you obey the Lord? Why did you rush for the loot and do exactly what God said not to?"
>
> "But I *have* obeyed the Lord," Saul insisted. "I did what he told me to; and I brought King Agag but killed everyone else. And it was only when my troops demanded it that I let them keep the best of the sheep and oxen and loot to sacrifice to the Lord."
>
> Samuel replied, "Has the Lord as much pleasure in your burnt offerings and sacrifices as in your obedience? Obedience is far better than sacrifice. He is much more interested in your listening to him than in your offering the fat of rams to him. For rebellion is as bad as the sin of witchcraft, and stubbornness is as bad as worshiping idols. And now because

you have rejected the word of Jehovah, he has rejected you from being king" (1 Samuel 15:17-23).

Have you been struggling with an attitude of rebelliousness or stubbornness? That can all change when you choose an attitude of obedience to what you know you need to be doing. No passing the buck like Saul did. Just obey.

Have you ever seen pictures or movies of wild stallions running through hills and mountains? They're beautiful and magnificent creatures—but they're good for nothing until they submit to the bit and the bridle. Only when a wild horse's energy and power become submissive and obedient to a rider does the horse become useful for service.

Have you been struggling against the bit and the bridle in your life? Have you been stubborn and rebellious? Do you want to become useful for service? Then you know what your prayer needs to be: "Lord, teach me to be submissive to Your leadership."

Submission is the willingness to give up our right
to ourselves, to freely surrender our insistence
on having our own way all the time.

MYLES MUNROE

Submission to duty and God gives the highest energy. He
who has done the greatest work on earth said that he
came down from heaven, not to do his own will, but the
will of Him who sent him. Whoever allies himself with
God is armed with all the forces of the invisible world.

JAMES FREEMAN CLARKE

Laughter Therapy

In her poem "Solitude," Ella Wheeler Wilcox wrote,

Laugh, and the world laughs with you;
Weep, and you weep alone;
For the sad old earth must borrow its mirth,
But has trouble enough of its own.

Laughter can help to change a negative attitude into a positive attitude, and laughter brings people together. Victor Borge once said, "Laughter is the closest distance between two people." A study in Norway suggests that people with a strong sense of humor outlive those who do not laugh much.[8]

The benefits of laughter include:

- Adding to Heart Health
- Aiding in Losing Calories
- Assisting with Creativity
- Boosting Immunity
- Clearing the Mind
- Decreasing Stress
- Easing Depression
- Improving Blood Flow
- Keeping Things in Perspective
- Lessening Inflammation
- Lowering Blood Pressure
- Producing Endorphins
- Promoting Bonding
- Reducing Conflict
- Relaxing the Body
- Seeing the Bright Side of Life
- Slowing Memory Loss
- Supporting Mood Change

There is nothing in the world so irresistibly contagious as laughter and good humor.

CHARLES DICKENS

The person who can bring the spirit of laughter into a room is indeed blessed.

BENNETT CERF

You can't deny laughter; when it comes, it plops down in your favorite chair and stays as long as it wants.

STEPHEN KING

*If you wish to glimpse inside a human soul and get to
know a man, don't bother analyzing his ways of being
silent, of talking, of weeping, of seeing how much he is
moved by noble ideas; you will get better results if you just
watch him laugh. If he laughs well, he's a good man.*

FYODOR DOSTOEVSKY

Robinson Crusoe Syndrome

In 1719, Daniel Defoe published the novel *Robinson Crusoe*—the
story of a man who is shipwrecked on a remote tropical desert island. He

lived on the island for 28 years. For much of
the story, Crusoe, is on the island all by himself. Although he gathers resources from the
shipwreck to make his life more comfortable,
he is often without human society and living
in loneliness.

Many people today face the Robinson
Crusoe Syndrome. Although human society
exists around them, they still feel a deep sense
of loneliness. They struggle with the negative
attitude of having few or no friends, and they feel alone. Do you know
anyone like that? Maybe you feel like that.

There is a difference between having acquaintances and having
friends. Some have suggested there are three categories of friends.

1. Some friends you know on a very casual basis. They are the
   hi-and-bye friends you spend almost no time with. They
   could make up about 20 percent of the casual friends you
   know.

2. You may spend more time with other friends without
   knowing them deeply—for example, people from work,
   people from church, or people you occasionally go out with.
   You might rub shoulders with them or have contact on an
   occasional to a frequent basis. This group would make up
   about 75 percent of the *normal friends* you know.

3. Lastly, you may have *intimate friends*. You have a mutual bond of affection with these people. They are friends you trust, like, and enjoy being with on an extended basis. These friends support, encourage, and sympathize with you. This small group makes up about 5 percent or less of your friendships.

When people struggle with the Robinson Crusoe Syndrome, it's not usually hi-and-bye or normal friends they are lacking; they long for intimate friends. They are lonely and long for someone close to open their hearts to. Do you have some intimate friends in your life?

Developing intimate friends takes time and common experience. It means nurturing a sincere interest in each other and an openness to share heartfelt needs with one another.

If you feel like you're on a desert island, then build a bridge to the mainland. Get to know some people and spend time together. A good place to start is with the normal friends you already know. As you think about this group of people, does anyone in particular come to mind with whom you would like to have a deeper relationship? If so, give them a call or send them a note. Put some effort into it.

If you don't know anyone like that, here are some ideas for meeting people.

- What groups could you join?
- What workshops or courses could expose you to more people?
- Are you open to accepting invitations to go out with friends?
- Are you open to becoming involved with volunteer or mission projects?
- Do you go to parties when invited?
- What church and community activities are you involved in?

Do you expect strangers to come to your house seeking you as a friend? Do you think they'll knock on the door and say, "I'm here to meet you"? You know it doesn't happen that way. To have a friend, you must become a friend. Friendship requires time.

For Robinson Crusoe, a native happens to show up on his island one Friday. Crusoe then names his new acquaintance Friday. They are not friends at first. They have to spend time together and face problems and difficulties together. They have to fight through dangerous events together. Only after all of that do they become intimate friends who would die for each other.

I'm pretty sure your version of Friday is not going to show up at your doorstep anytime soon, so the ball is in your court. Consider asking God to give you a new attitude about looking for and developing friendships.

You can make more friends in two months by becoming
interested in other people than you can in two years
by trying to get other people interested in you.

DALE CARNEGIE

The best way to cheer yourself is to try to cheer somebody else up.

MARK TWAIN

Friendship, of itself a holy tie, is made more sacred by adversity.

JOHN DRYDEN

Friendship is like a bank account. You can't continue
to draw on it without making deposits.

R.E. PHILLIPS

Memories

Lewis Carroll gives us some insight about how to deal with negative memories that keep reminding us of past hurts. In *Through the Looking Glass*, the king is talking about a problem he faced. The queen responds with an answer.

"The horror of that moment," the King went on. "I shall never, *never* forget!"

"You will, though," the Queen said, "if you don't make a memorandum of it."

We are all prone to making a memorandum of the hurts, disappointments, and discontents we've experienced; but to gain a new attitude, we must let go of the old attitude.

Don't tell your problems to people. Eighty percent don't care and the other twenty percent are glad you have them.

LOU HOLTZ

Forget what hurt you but never forget what it taught you.

UNKNOWN

Everybody's got a past. The past does not equal the future unless you live there.

TONY ROBBINS

Letting go helps us to live in a more peaceful state of mind and helps restore our balance. It allows others to be responsible for themselves and for us to take our hands off situations that do not belong to us. This frees us from unnecessary stress.

MELODY BEATTIE

Don't dwell on what went wrong. Instead, focus on what to do next. Spend your energies on moving forward toward finding the answer.

DENIS WAITLEY

Some people believe holding on and hanging in there are signs of great strength. However, there are times when it takes much more strength to know when to let go and then do it.

ANN LANDERS

Attitude Land Mines

Danger! Do everything you can to avoid, step over, and move away from *attitude land mines.* When they blow up, your emotions become out of proportion to the events going on in your life.

Attitude land mines injure your ego, mess up your thinking, and keep you from making positive choices for healthy behavior. When attitude land mines explode, they can:

- make you sad
- make you feel dull
- make you moody
- make you feel foolish
- make you unhappy
- make you regretful
- make you feel unworthy
- make you feel depressed

- make you feel inadequate
- make you pessimistic
- make you feel despondent
- make you feel melancholy
- make you hate your body
- make you feel discouraged
- make you feel unimportant
- make you keep a diary of all your failures
- make you fearful of saying the wrong thing
- make you quiet, timid, or shy
- make you accept blame for everything going on
- make you hesitant to share your thoughts and opinions
- make you feel uncomfortable in crowds or groups of people
- make you set impossible standards of perfection for yourself
- make you compare yourself to others
- make you answer to names like *stupid, incompetent, ugly, selfish, weak,* and *fearful*

Chronic self-doubt is a symptom of the core belief: "I'm not good enough." We adopt these types of limiting beliefs in response to our family and childhood experiences, and they become rooted in the subconscious... When we understand the roots of self-doubt, we then have the ability to take action to override it.

LAUREN MACKLER

Psychotherapy is what God has been secretly doing for centuries by other names; that is, he searches through our personal history and heals what needs to be healed—the wounds of childhood or our own self-inflicted wounds.

THOMAS KEATING

Faith in the gospel restructures our motivations, our self-understanding, our identity, and our view of the world. It changes our hearts. Behavioral compliance to rules without heart change will be superficial and fleeting... We can only change permanently as we take the gospel more deeply into our understanding and into our hearts. We must feed on the gospel, as it were, digesting it and making it part of ourselves. That is how we grow.

TIMOTHY KELLER

Alice in Wonderland

Lewis Carroll addresses the subject of motivation in *Alice's Adventures in Wonderland*. In the following scene, Alice is lost and needs direction. She asks the Cheshire cat:

"Would you tell me please, which way I ought to go from here?"

"That depends a good deal on where you want to get to," said the Cat.

"I don't much care where—" said Alice.

"Then it doesn't matter which way you go," said the Cat.

Many people believe that motivation helps to determine your goals in life. However, that's not how it works. It's just the opposite. Your goals determine your motivation. If you don't have any goals, you certainly will not have any motivation to reach them.

I have met a number of people who say, "I don't have any goals." Is it any wonder they are struggling to find direction in life? What are your goals? Are you happy? Are you happy with your attitudes? Are you happy in your relationships? Are you happy with the emotions you are dealing with? If not, why? Would you like to be moving in another direction?

Generally, we don't change our behavior until we *hurt* enough to change. If you're satisfied where you are, you have little motivation to change. If you're not satisfied, then you will set goals for change that motivate you.

The Cheshire cat is here to ask you the same question: "Where do you want to go?"

Your life does not get better by chance, it gets better by change.

JIM ROHN

Excellence is never an accident. It is always the result of high intention, sincere effort, and intelligent execution; it represents the wise choice of many alternatives— choice, not chance, determines your destiny.

ARISTOTLE

Goals are not only absolutely necessary to motivate us. They are essential to really keep us alive.

ROBERT H. SCHULLER

In any moment of decision, the best thing you can do is the right thing, the next best thing is the wrong thing, and the worst thing you can do is nothing.

UNKNOWN

Law of Flexible Planning

The law of flexible planning says, "Whatever can go wrong, will go wrong." Therefore, plan on it going wrong—so when it goes wrong, you can say, "That was my plan."

You may be thinking: *What are you really saying then?*

I'm saying: "Relax. Chill. Ease up a little." Not everything in life will work out the way you want it to. Developing an attitude of flexibility will help even the most uptight person learn to accept change.

> *Progress is impossible without change, and those who*
> *cannot change their minds cannot change anything.*
>
> GEORGE BERNARD SHAW

Criticism

Do you like to be criticized? Do you know anyone who does? I have yet to find someone who can say, "I love to be criticized."

What is criticism? To criticize is to give an opinion based on the perceived faults or mistakes of another—an expression indicating judgment and disapproval and is usually unfavorable.

You may say, "Wait a minute. Isn't it possible to give constructive criticism to help a person?" I really question that possibility. Underlying constructive criticism is an air of control, censure, and condemnation, which are hard to receive.

Although it's good to make changes in bad attitudes and behavior, the crucial part is *how* those changes are suggested to another individual. Remember that not all criticism is true and valid. Often those who criticize you are simply venting their own fears, angers, and jealousies with a desire to control, hurt, or get revenge. This type of criticism has inspired proverbs, such as: "The dogs bark, and the caravan rolls on." (Don't pay attention to a lot of complaining.) "When you get kicked by a donkey, you have to consider the source." (Consider the character and motivation of the antagonist.)

You would be better off spending your time around positive people with healthy attitudes instead of people who are filled with complaints and disgust. You're already hard enough on yourself; you don't need to add someone else's negativity to your already heavy load.

Theodore Roosevelt addressed this concept when he said,

> It is not the critic who counts: not the man who points out how the strong man stumbles or where the doer of deeds could have done better. The credit belongs to the man who is actually in the arena, whose face is marred by dust and sweat and blood, who strives valiantly…who, at the best, knows, in the end, the triumph of high achievement, and who, at the worst, if he fails, at least he fails while daring greatly.

> *The way we respond to criticism pretty much depends on the way we respond to praise. If praise humbles us, then criticism will build us up. But if praise inflates us, then criticism will crush us; and both responses lead to our defeat.*
>
> WARREN W. WIERSBE

> *If I care to listen to every criticism, let alone act on them, then this shop may as well be closed for all other businesses. I have learned to do my best, and if the end result is good, then I do not care for any criticism, but if the end result is not good, then even the praise of ten angels would not make the difference.*
>
> ABRAHAM LINCOLN

Golf Course Mentality

Have you ever heard someone say, "I can't hardly wait to retire; I'm going to relax and spend my time at the golf course"? Really? How do you think that's going to work out on a daily basis?

One of the reasons we have so many old, crotchety, and grumpy men and women is because they have nothing to do or live for. They become lonely, bored, annoyed, and resentful. There are three major reasons that older people get depressed: from listening to ABC, NBC, and CBS.

In retirement it's important to develop habits of excitement, creativity, and contribution. You need to become excited about having more time to develop interests and hobbies that you once put on the back burner. You can travel, develop a new skill, go back to school, or volunteer for community projects or mission opportunities. You could become a teacher, mentor, or tutor. You don't want to become a slug or couch potato.

Before you retired, you experienced mental stimulation, involvement with people, and a sense of contribution. For your retirement to be a happy and successful one, those three things need to continue. There is no greater joy than to give back to others some of the blessings you have received.

> *I don't know what your destiny will be, but one thing I know: the only ones among you who will be really happy are those who will have sought and found how to serve.*
>
> **ALBERT SCHWEITZER**

> *You have not lived today until you have done something for someone who can never repay you.*
>
> **JOHN BUNYAN**

> *It is hard to feel bad about yourself when you are doing something good for someone else. There are a lot of ways to lift your self-esteem, but making a positive difference in another's life has got to be my best leadership guidance. Serving others and working to add value to them will lift your spirits in a way that nothing else will. Trust me on this one.*
>
> **JOHN C. MAXWELL**

Turning Gold into Lead

According to Greek mythology, King Midas was granted one wish from the gods. He was very greedy and asked that whatever he touched be turned to gold. His wish was granted. When Midas decided to try out his new gift, he touched a rock that became solid gold. He was beside himself with joy at the possibility of becoming the wealthiest person who ever lived. He touched flowers, and they became gold. He touched a horse, and it became gold. For the rest of the day he touched as many things as he could, and each one turned to gold.

He then went up to one of his guards and asked him to protect his hoard of gold. In the process of telling the guard what to do, Midas put his hand on the guard's shoulder. You

TURNING GOLD INTO LEAD

guessed it: He turned to gold. With that, Midas laughed and thought to himself, *Well, that's more gold for me.*

After a hard day of turning everything to gold, he became hungry. He went for dinner, and everything he picked up turned to gold. No longer did he have any food to eat. It then dawned on him that the gift from the gods was, in reality, a curse. With no food, he would die before enjoying his fortune.

While he was sitting there in fear and sadness, his young daughter came up to give her father a kiss. As soon as she did, she turned to gold.

Midas ran to the gods and asked for his gift to be removed from him. His wish was granted but not without consequences. As a punishment for disagreeing with the gods, Midas was given donkey ears.

When people have a negative and pessimistic attitude, everywhere they look, whatever they say, and how they respond is colored with criticism and judgment. They take basic golden blessings and turn them into lead. And in the process of disapproval, condemnation, and denunciation, they turn themselves into donkeys.

To turn lead back into gold, follow the advice of Paul the apostle in Philippians 4:4-9.

> Always be full of joy in the Lord; I say it again, rejoice! Let everyone see that you are unselfish and considerate in all you do. Remember that the Lord is coming soon. Don't worry about anything; instead, pray about everything; tell God your needs, and don't forget to thank him for his answers. If you do this, you will experience God's peace, which is far more wonderful than the human mind can understand. His peace will keep your thoughts and your hearts quiet and at rest as you trust in Christ Jesus.

And now, brothers, as I close this letter, let me say this one more thing: Fix your thoughts on what is true and good and right. Think about things that are pure and lovely, and dwell on the fine, good things in others. Think about all you can praise God for and be glad about. Keep putting into practice all you learned from me and saw me doing, and the God of peace will be with you.

This is real gold!

Dear God,

I realize that many times I have to make a decision with little information and facts. Please give me clarity of thinking and the courage to make important decisions. I want You to direct the paths of my life. Help me to be submissive and not rebellious in following You. Help me to not dwell on the problems of life and criticisms from other people. Teach me to be flexible and to develop a positive attitude rather than a negative outlook on life. And God, please help me to learn to laugh and enjoy this wonderful life You gave me.

Amen

Attitude Is a Choice...So Pick a Good One.

ATTITUDE TOOL KIT

One Year of Positive Behavior Changes

Smile Month

Spend the next 30 days attempting to smile and look into the eyes of at least five people a day—then try for more. Keep a daily log. For every person under five a day that you didn't smile at, put one dollar into what we'll call the "Good Attitude Jar."

Proverbs Month

Read one chapter a day from the book of Proverbs in the Bible. There are 31 chapters, so pick a month that has 31 days in it. Each day, find a verse from the chapter and write it on a three-by-five-inch index card. Review the card at least three times a day. For every day that you don't read a chapter, put a dollar into the Good Attitude Jar.

Discipline Month

Spend the next 30 days getting your act together. Clean your house, make your bed every day, and clean out your garage. Tidy your desk, drawers in the house, and other areas that need to be organized. You've been putting it off long enough. For every day you don't make your bed, put another dollar in the Good Attitude Jar.

Affirmation Month

Throughout this book, many quotations and affirmations have been included to challenge and encourage you. During the next 30 days, choose quotes that impress you, encourage you, or challenge you and write them on a three-by-five-inch index card. These quotes can come from other places than *Attitude Is a Choice*. Take the cards with you and review them. Put them on your refrigerator or the mirror in your bathroom as reminders. Put them on the sun visor in your car or on your desk at work. If someone asks you about your cards, explain to them what you are attempting to do and how the affirmations affect your attitude. Set your alarm on your phone, and every two hours, pull out a card and read the affirmation. For every day you don't review your affirmations, put one dollar in the Good Attitude Jar.

Good Eating Month

Oh no! Here comes one month to test your willpower and control. We all know it is important to eat good, nourishing food for our health. For the next 30 days, test your ability to say no to extra snacks apart from a dessert at mealtimes. This includes sugary snacks at coffee breaks, in between meals, and in the late evening. Every time you violate the rules or break down and eat a snack, put one dollar in the Good Attitude Jar.

Patience Month

Would you like to have more patience? If you answered yes, you're really saying you would like to have more trials, difficulties, and problems in life. Why do I say that? It's because you don't need patience when everything is going your way. You need patience when things are going wrong. For the next 30 days, work on your patience by controlling your frustrations and temper. You are a work in progress, but every time you lose your patience or make a negative comment out of anger or frustration, put one dollar in the Good Attitude Jar.

Reading Month

Over the next 30 days, discipline yourself to read at least two self-help books on any subject of interest to you. "But I don't read books," you may say. Precisely the point. You won't develop or expand your knowledge if you maintain your present behavior. You won't die by reading a book. In fact, you might even learn something of use for you. Imagine that. For every book you do not read during the next 30 days, put five dollars in the Good Attitude Jar.

Exercise Month

During the next 30 days, begin walking as an exercise. Start off by walking around the block or another short distance. Don't try to gauge the distance as much as the amount of time you are walking. Begin with a 16-minute walk. Walk eight minutes in one direction, then turn around and walk back. Each day, see if you can add more minutes to your walk. You can also add "Touch Your Toes Month" to this challenge. At the beginning of the walk, spend a few minutes attempting to touch your toes. At the end of the walk, try to touch your toes again. You will be surprised how much closer you can get to your toes in a month. For each day you don't go for a walk, put a dollar in the Good Attitude Jar.

Clean Up Your Mouth Month

For the next 30 days, work on your speech. This means cutting out the swearing, the criticizing, the sarcasm, the complaining, the gossiping, the negative comments, and the put-downs of other people. This may be your most expensive month. You'll get the message—painfully. For each time you don't control your speech, put a dollar in the Good Attitude Jar. For some, you may have to reduce it to 50 cents or a quarter—or otherwise go broke.

Encouragement Month

For the next 30 days, your assignment is to be an encourager. Write thank-you notes or speak words of appreciation or support to your family, friends, coworkers, or even strangers. You will need to do this for at least three people a day. For every person under three per day, put one dollar in the Good Attitude Jar.

Communication Month

For the next 30 days, focus on improving your communication skills. Begin by really listening to people. Listen to what they are saying (their words) and the tone of voice they are using. Take note of the body language they use in their communication. Begin to use clarifying questions to be sure you have accurate understanding. When you need to talk with someone about an important issue, be alert to timing. Ask yourself: "Is this the best time to talk to them, or would another time be better?" For every time you become aware that you are not using the best communication skills, put one dollar in the Good Attitude Jar.

Kindness Month

For the next 30 days, make it your practice to do something positive and out of the ordinary. The goal is to make someone else's life easier. This could include washing the dishes, cleaning the house, doing extra yard work, helping with homework, assisting a friend or neighbor, or helping an elderly person or single parent. It could include community service, mission work, or random acts of kindness. Consider this a "passing forward" of the various acts of kindness others have shown to you over the years. Each time you pass up an opportunity to do a good deed, put another dollar in the Good Attitude Jar.

The Good Attitude Jar

What's the purpose of the Good Attitude Jar? The jar is simply a visual and financial reminder of your desire to make positive attitude changes in your life. Every time you fall short of your goals, you pay a "fine" into the jar. The negative reinforcement should help you stay on track to accomplish your goals month by month.

What should you do with the money collected in the

Good Attitude Jar? Give it away to a needy person or family, a charity, or a missions project. The jar is a way of encouraging you to work on the attitude changes you would like to make—while also helping someone else's life to be a little easier.

Being on Time Week

For this week, make every effort to be on time for appointments. To be consistently late displays an attitude of selfishness.

> *Arriving late was a way of saying that your own time was more valuable than the time of the person who waited for you.*
>
> KAREN JOY FOWLER

> *Punctuality is closely related to faithfulness and dependability. Being tardy can be linked to uninterest, apathy, slothfulness and procrastination.*
>
> STERLING W. SILL

> *It is difficult to prove yourself reliable when people are required to wait for you.*
>
> WES FESLER

> *Being on time to appointments and meetings is a phase of self-discipline and an evidence of self-respect. Punctuality is a courteous compliment the intelligent person pays to his associates.*
>
> MARVIN J. ASHTON

Special People Week

For a week, treat everyone you meet, without a single exception, as the most important person on earth. You will find that they will begin treating you the same way. It's a real attitude boost.

> *My mom always used to say that average people are the most special people in the world. And that's why God made so many.*
>
> MICHAEL SCOTT, *THE OFFICE*

Get Out of Yourself Week

Talk to at least one stranger a day for two weeks. Then write down what you discovered.

> *The best antidote I know for worry is work. The best cure for weariness is the challenge of helping someone who is even more tired. One of the great ironies of life is this: He or she who serves almost always benefits more than he or she who is served.*
>
> **GORDON B. HINCKLEY**

Sneak Week

Pass it forward. Do something or give something to someone without them asking for it. And be sure to keep it a secret so they will have no one to praise but God, who answered their prayer *through you.*

> *Happiness comes from spiritual wealth, not material wealth...Happiness comes from giving, not getting...If we try hard to bring happiness to others, we cannot stop it from coming to us also...To get joy we must give it and to keep joy we must scatter it.*
>
> **JOHN TEMPLETON**

Mood Week

Are you happy with the attitude or mood you have been displaying to others? Decide to display a particular positive mood or attitude for one entire week. Being happy would be a good start.

> *The predominant quality of successful people is optimism...Your level of optimism is the very best predictor of how happy, healthy, wealthy, and long-lived you will be.*
>
> **BRIAN TRACY**

Blessing List

Make a list of all your blessings. Review it every night before you go to sleep for 30 days.

*Count your blessings. Once you realize how valuable you
are and how much you have going for you, the smiles will
return, the sun will break out, the music will play, and you
will finally be able to move forward in the life that God
intended for you with grace, strength, courage, and confidence.*

OG MANDINO

Success Diary

Keep a track record of positive actions you've taken and goals you've reached. When you make a grocery list, you mark *off* the items purchased to ensure you picked up everything you needed. In a list of accomplishments, you don't *take off* anything. You add to the list your successes, victories, and attainments. Make sure to list the small achievements along with the large achievements. The practice will motivate you to reach even more goals, targets, and dreams.

*Success is not the key to happiness. Happiness is the key to
success. If you love what you are doing, you will be successful.*

ALBERT SCHWEITZER

Ten-Minute Clearing of Unwanted / Unnecessary E-mails—No wandering around at other Internet sites.

Ten-Minute Contact—Select an individual working under you or someone working with you. Find out how they are doing, what's going on with their family, and ask if there is anything you can do to make their job easier.

Ten-Minute Review of Goal Sheet—Take a few minutes to review your goal sheet and cross off accomplishments and add new goals to pursue.

Ten-Minute Change of Pace—Go outside and get some sunshine and fresh air. Clear your head; ponder a problem; review a blessing; take a moment to pray for someone.

Ten-Minute Review of Financial Status—This will help to keep you from overspending.

The Super Simple Budget

Monthly Income

1. Salary or wages— ("Take-home" after deductions) $_____

2. Salary or wages— ("Take-home" after deductions) $_____

3. Other income (only list regular monthly income) $_____

4. TOTAL CASH ("Take-home" income per month) $_____

List which pay period you want to pay bills "A" through "P"

Fixed Monthly Expenses	**First Pay Period**	**Second Pay Period**
A. Giving	$_____ $_____	$_____
B. House Payment/Rent	$_____ $_____	$_____
C. Gas and Electricity	$_____ $_____	$_____
D. Water and Garbage	$_____ $_____	$_____
E. Phone	$_____ $_____	$_____
F. Food and Household Items	$_____ $_____	$_____
G. Car Payment	$_____ $_____	$_____
H. Gasoline	$_____ $_____	$_____
I. Car Insurance	$_____	
J. Life Insurance	$_____	
K. Loans	$_____	
L. Union Dues	$_____	
M._____	$_____	Total Cash Line 4 $_____
N._____	$_____	
O._____	$_____	Subtract Total
P. _____	$_____	Fixed Expenses
5. **Total Fixed Expenses**	$_____	$_____
6. **Total**—[Flexible or Controllable Monies— Less Fixed Expenses]		$_____

Miscellaneous Expenses to Be Paid From the Monies on Line Six

A. Doctor, Dentist, Drugs	$_____	Total
B. Education, Lessons	$_____	Controllable
C. Home Improvements	$_____	Monies From
D. Car Maintenance	$_____	Line 6
E. Allowances, Mad Money	$_____	$_____
F. Charge Accounts	$_____	
G. Appliances	$_____	
H. Babysitting	$_____	
I. Subscriptions	$_____	
J. Clothing	$_____	
K. Gifts	$_____	
L. Furniture	$_____	
M. Entertainment, Recreation	$_____	
N. Saving Accounts	$_____	
O. Incidentals	$_____	
P. _____	$_____	
Q. _____	$_____	
R. Buffer or Emergency Monies	$_____	
Total Miscellaneous Expenses	$_____	

Money... is like a beautiful thoroughbred horse—very powerful and always in action, but unless this horse is trained when very young, it will be an out-of-control and dangerous animal when it grows to maturity.

DAVE RAMSEY

Attitude Is a Choice...So Pick a Good One.

19

ATTITUDE ISSUES

As we learned from Charles Kettering, "A problem well stated is a problem half solved." To help maintain a positive attitude, it's helpful to determine the possible conflict issue that might be the root of the problem. Once that is discovered, those discussing the issue can stay on track more easily, without getting lost in conversations that cloud the most important issue. Focus on resolving this base conflict before expanding into other issues. Then try to deal with one issue at a time, working through everything until an understanding forms between the parties. Together, attempt to reach a conclusion that benefits all involved individuals. Peace, harmony, and reconciliation would be the goal.

- Accountability issue
- Aptitude/ability issue
- Attitude issue
- Barrier issue
- Belief issue
- Communication issue
- Control issue
- Corruption issue
- Credibility issue
- Criminal issue
- Cultural issue
- Disciplinary issue
- Discord issue
- Ethics issue
- Failure issue
- Forgiveness issue
- Goals issue
- Integrity issue
- Invasion of space issue
- Judgment issue
- Knowledge issue
- Lack of control issue
- Leadership issue
- Mental health issue
- Methods issue
- Morals issue

- Perception issue
- Personal preference issue
- Physical attack issue
- Policy issue
- Power issue
- Procedure issue
- Rebellion issue
- Repeated behavioral issue
- Resource issue
- Responsibility issue
- Scheduling issue
- Silence or withdrawal issue
- Standards issue
- Timing issue
- Tolerance issue
- Traditions issue
- Training issue
- Transparency issue
- Trust issue
- Values issue
- Verbal attack issue
- Violation of rights issue

Attitude Is a Choice...So Pick a Good One.

20

BAD ATTITUDE TRIGGERS

Place a check mark in boxes that tend to trigger
a bad attitude in your spirit.

☐ Accidents

☐ Angry comments

☐ Authority figures

☐ Bad day at work

☐ Being brunt of gossip

☐ Being depressed

☐ Being hungry

☐ Being ignored

☐ Being jilted

☐ Being lied to

☐ Being lonely

☐ Being rejected

☐ Being tired

☐ Bossy people

☐ Breaking something

☐ Condescending talk

☐ Constant complainers

☐ Critical people

☐ Feeling guilty

☐ Feeling unattractive

☐ Financial worries

☐ Getting a speeding ticket

☐ Grouchy people

☐ Having something stolen

☐ Indecisive people

☐ Job discrimination

☐ Judgmental people

☐ Know-it-alls

☐ Losers

☐ Losing something

☐ Loss of control

☐ Loss of job

☐ Loss of trust

☐ Lousy service

☐ Monday mornings

☐ Nosy people

☐ Not fitting in

☐ Not getting your way

- ☐ Other people being late
- ☐ People laughing at you
- ☐ People making excuses
- ☐ People who blame others
- ☐ People who bully
- ☐ People who hurt feelings
- ☐ People who tailgate
- ☐ Poor service
- ☐ Power hungry people
- ☐ Rude people
- ☐ Self-defeating talk
- ☐ Sickness in family
- ☐ Slow talkers
- ☐ Slow walkers
- ☐ Stepping on dog droppings
- ☐ Too little sleep
- ☐ Traffic delays
- ☐ Under time pressure
- ☐ Unfair situations
- ☐ Unhealthy comparisons
- ☐ Unrealistic expectations
- ☐ Unresolved conflict
- ☐ Weather
- ☐ Your child's disobedience

Attitude Is a Choice...So Pick a Good One.

21

BAD ATTITUDE BUSTERS

*I don't have any bad habits. They might be bad habits
for other people, but they're all right for me.*

EUBIE BLAKE

1. I tend to bring my problems to work with me.
   How about leaving them at home today?

2. I don't think people like me.
   Have you ever thought there might be a reason why?

3. When things go wrong, I blame others.
   Gee, you must really be liked.

4. I talk to other people about my problems.
   Oh, good. Now others can be bored too.

5. I get angry and mad often.
   Is that working for you?

6. I hate slow drivers and people who cut in front of my car.
   *You'll have to forgive them for driving on your road. They didn't
   know King Me-Me was behind them.*

7. I can't stand people who won't listen to me.
   Sure. As if you always listen.

8. I don't like my spouse.
   You're even. They probably don't like you either.

9. Why do I have these negative guilt feelings?
   Maybe because your conscience says you're guilty.

10. I hate my job.
    Hello! Get a new one.

11. My boss is an idiot.
    It's sure good he has the only smart person alive working for him.

12. The weather is terrible.
    Please forgive the weather. It forgot to change for you.

13. I can't stand it when people don't keep their commitments.
    You should write a book on how you have always kept your commitments.

14. I don't seem to have any friends.
    Maybe you should try to be one for a change.

15. I have bad luck.
    Maybe you missed the sign that says, "Hard work brings luck."

16. I don't like myself.
    You're not alone.

17. Who's responsible for this mess?
    Turn around and look in the mirror.

18. I've lost my motivation.
    The light has finally dawned.

19. Things aren't going right for me.
    Should I bring balloons to your pity party?

20. They're always making snide comments about others.
    It takes one to know one.

21. I always hear people criticizing others.
    It might be the echo of your whining?

22. I can't seem to get over my divorce.
    Yeah, it's hard to do when you keep talking and moaning about it.

23. My relatives are terrible.
    It's too bad they can't be perfect like you are.

24. I always search for truth.
    What do you usually find? Faults? Just asking.

25. Nobody seems to care for me.
    Maybe they're having a tough time wading through all your whimpering and sniveling.

26. I can't stand gossips. I only say what's good about people.
    Let me guess: You're going to tell me to listen carefully to this information because it's really good.

27. I struggle with impatience. How do I develop more patience?
    Ask God to bring you more problems. You don't need patience when you're problem-free.

28. How do I go about having a good day?
    Stop your bellyaching and complaining for a while.

29. What should I do about my bad attitude?
    How about putting on your big boy or big girl pants—then growing up?

30. I can never do anything right.
    I can think of one right thing. You started reading this book.

> *The best cure for one's bad tendencies is to see them in action in another person.*
>
> ALAIN DE BOTTON

Attitude Is a Choice...So Pick a Good One.

22

ATTITUDE CHECKS FOR BROKENNESS

- Am I willing to let go of my dreams and ambitions if such is God's will?
- Am I defensive when accused, criticized, or misunderstood?
- Am I coveting what others have instead of waiting for heaven's rewards?
- Am I forgiving when offended, with or without apology?
- Am I complaining or arguing because of unsurrendered rights?
- Am I thinking of others first out of love?
- Am I proudly appearing that I am always right or know all the answers?
- Am I practicing the spiritual disciplines: reading God's Word, prayer, fasting, solitude, simplicity, meeting together with others, giving of earthly possessions, time, service, etc.?
- Am I being silent regarding self-promotion and letting God do my public relations?
- Am I daily saying, "God, whatever it takes, I'm willing to submit to Your leadership"?
- Am I expressing joy in the difficulties that serve to refine me?
- Am I taking risks out of obedience to Christ, or am I giving in to fear, pride, or denial?

Attitude Is a Choice...So Pick a Good One.

23

POSITIVE ATTITUDE TRAITS

Words in bold are foundational.

- Alert—Thinking clearly and intellectually active.
- Ambitious—Having desire and determination to achieve success.
- Attentive—Showing careful attention to the comfort or wishes of others.
- Compassionate—Showing sympathy and concern for others.
- Confident—Certain in one's worth, abilities, and qualities.
- **Convicted**—Confidently sharing thoughts, opinions, and firmly held beliefs.
- **Courageous**—Able to do things that one fears.
- Creative—Showing inventiveness and use of imagination.
- Curious—Showing a strong desire to know or learn new things.
- Dependable—Being trustworthy and reliable.
- **Diligent**—Working carefully and persistently.
- **Disciplined**—Doing what one should do (even if one doesn't feel like it).
- Dutiful—Conscientiously or obediently fulfilling one's duty.
- Encouraging—Giving others support, confidence, or hope.
- Energetic—Showing or involving great activity or vitality.
- Faithful—Remaining loyal and steadfast.
- Flexible—Ready and able to adapt to different circumstances.

- Forgiving—Feeling no anger or resentment to offenses or mistakes.
- Friendly—Being favorable and serviceable to others.
- Generous—Ready to give more than necessary or expected.
- Hardworking—Working with energy and commitment.
- Honest—Free of deceit; truthful and sincere.
- Honorable—Knowing and doing what is morally right.
- Hopeful—Feeling or inspiring optimism about a future event.
- **Humble**—Having a modest or low view of one's importance.
- Independent—Thinking and acting for oneself.
- Industrious—Diligent and hardworking.
- Kind—Being friendly, generous, and considerate.
- Listening—Taking notice of and making an effort to hear others.
- Logical—Acting based on clear, sound reasoning.
- Loving—Feeling and showing deep, selfless affection for others.
- Loyal—Showing firm and constant support or allegiance.
- Neat—Tidy, smart, or well-organized.
- Open-minded—Accepting of and receptive to change or new ideas.
- **Optimistic**—Positive outlook with a confident, cheerful, and enthusiastic spirit.
- Organized—Structured, systematic, and good at planning.
- Passionate—Having, showing, or driven by strong feelings or beliefs.
- Patient—Waiting without getting tired of waiting.

- Persistent—Continuing firmly despite difficulty or opposition.
- Polite—Acting respectfully and considerately.
- Punctual—Doing things at agreed or proper times.
- Purposeful—Showing determination or resolve.
- Rational—Thinking and acting in accordance with reason or logic.
- Reasonable—Having sound judgment; fair and sensible.
- Reliable—Consistently good in quality or performance.
- Respectful—Showing regard for the feelings, wishes, or rights of others.
- Self-controlled—Managing emotions and desires well in difficult situations.
- Sincere—Free from pretense or deceit.
- Strong—Not easily disturbed, upset, or affected.
- Thrifty—Using resources carefully and not wastefully.
- Trustworthy—Able to be relied on; honest or truthful.
- Truthful—Telling or expressing the truth; honest.
- Unselfish—Putting the needs or wishes of others before one's own.
- Upright—Good, reliable, full of integrity
- Valiant—Possessing or showing courage or determination.
- Warm—Showing enthusiasm, affection, or kindness.
- Wise—Showing experience, knowledge, and good judgment.

Attitude Is a Choice...So Pick a Good One.

24

CAN-DO ATTITUDES

Can't-Do	Can-Do
We've never done it before	We have the opportunity to be first
It's too complicated	Let's look at it from a different angle
We don't have the resources	Necessity is the mother of invention
It will never work	We'll give it a try
There's not enough time	We'll reevaluate our priorities
We already tried it	We learned from the experience
There's no way it'll work	We can make it work
It's a waste of time	Think of the possibilities
It's a waste of money	The investment will be worth it
We don't have the expertise	Let's network with the experts
We can't compete	We'll get a jump on the competition
Our vendors won't go for it	Let's show them the opportunities
It's good enough	There is always room for improvement
We don't have enough money	Maybe there's something we can cut
We're understaffed	We're a lean, mean machine
We don't have enough room	Temporary space may be an option
It will never fly	We'll never know until we try
We don't have the equipment	Maybe we can sub it out

It's not going to be any better	We'll try it one more time
It can't be done	It'll be a challenge
No one communicates	Let's open the communication channels
I don't have any idea	I will come up with some alternatives
Let somebody else deal with it	I'm ready to learn something new
We're always changing direction	We're in touch with our customers
It's too radical of a change	Let's take a chance
It takes too long for approval	We'll walk it through the system
Our customers won't buy it	We'll do better at educating the buyers
It doesn't fit us	We should look at it
It's contrary to policy	Anything is possible
It's not my job	I'll be glad to take the responsibility
I can't	I can

Attitude Is a Choice…So Pick a Good One.

25

GOD'S SECRET FORMULA FOR CHANGING YOUR ATTITUDE

Philippians 4:4-9

COMMAND Always be full of joy in the Lord; I say it again, rejoice!

COMMAND Let everyone see that you are unselfish and considerate in all you do.

MOTIVATION Remember that the Lord is coming soon.

COMMAND Don't worry about anything; instead, pray about everything; tell God your needs, and don't forget to thank him for his answers.

A PROMISE If you do this, you will experience God's peace,

A GUARANTEE which is far more wonderful than the human mind can understand. His peace will keep your thoughts and your hearts quiet and at rest as you trust in Christ Jesus.

CLOSING And now, dear brothers, as I close this letter,

THOUGHT let me say this one more thing:

COMMAND Fix your thoughts on what is true and good and right.

COMMAND Think about things that are pure and lovely, and dwell on the fine, good things in others.

COMMAND   Think about all you can praise God for and be glad about.

COMMAND   Keep putting into practice all you learned from me and saw me doing,

PROMISE   and the God of peace will be with you.

Attitude Is a Choice...So Pick a Good One

26

THE BIBLE'S ATTITUDE ON OVER 270 TOPICS

ABILITY (GOD'S)
2 Corinthians 1:12
2 Corinthians 9:8
Ephesians 3:20
Hebrews 2:18
Jude 24-25

ABORTION
2 Chronicles 28:1-8
Psalm 71:5-6
Psalm 139:1-24
Jeremiah 1:5
Luke 1:41

ABUSIVE BEHAVIOR
Romans 12:10
Romans 12:18-19
1 Corinthians 10:31
1 Thessalonians 5:15
James 1:20

ACCOUNTABILITY
Joshua 7:1-15
Judges 6:1-16
Ecclesiastes 12:13-14
Romans 14:1-22

ACTIONS
Ezekiel 18:30
Psalm 26:2

2 Corinthians 13:5
Galatians 6:4
James 3:13
1 John 3:19-22

ADMONITION
John 5:39-40
Colossians 1:28
Colossians 3:16
1 Thessalonians 4:18
Hebrews 12:12-15

ADULTERY
Exodus 20:14
Isaiah 1:1-31
Hosea 1:1-11
Malachi 2:13-16
Matthew 5:27-32
Matthew 15:19
Matthew 19:9
Luke 16:16-18
John 8:1-11
1 Corinthians 6:9-11

ADVICE
Psalm 32:8
Psalm 119:24
Proverbs 1:1-19
Proverbs 3
Proverbs 6:20-35

Proverbs 10:1-32
Proverbs 15:22
Mark 10:17-31

ADVERSITY
Ruth 1:14
2 Samuel 15:21
Job 2:11
Proverbs 17:17
Proverbs 18:24
Proverbs 19:7
Proverbs 27:10

AFFECTIONS
Deuteronomy 4:9
Psalm 139:23-24
Proverbs 4: 23-27
Proverbs 22:5
Proverbs 23:19
Proverbs 28:26
Mark 14:38
Hebrews 12:15

AGGRESSION
2 Chronicles 20:12
Psalm 140:1-2, 12-13
Isaiah 2:4
Isaiah 54:14
Matthew 5:38-48
Ephesians 6:10-18
James 3:17

AID
Psalm 9:12
Psalm 18:2
Psalm 20:1-9
Psalm 41:4

Psalm 46:1
Psalm 91:15
Psalm 119:71
Psalm 138:7
Nahum 1:7

ALCOHOLISM
Genesis 9:21-23
Genesis 19:31-36
1 Samuel 25:36-38
Proverbs 20:1
Proverbs 23:29-35
Isaiah 5:11
Isaiah 28:7

AMBITION
Proverbs 23:23
Matthew 13:44-46
Matthew 16:26
Mark 10:35-38, 41-45
Luke 16:8
Philippians 3:7-12
James 3:14-16

ANGER
Genesis 4:5-7
Proverbs 14:17, 29
Proverbs 15:18
Proverbs 19:11, 19
Proverbs 20:3
Proverbs 22:24
Proverbs 25:28
Proverbs 29:11, 22
Matthew 5:21-26
Ephesians 4:26-32
James 1:19-20
James 3:6

ANXIETY
Psalm 16:11
Psalm 37:1, 7
Psalm 94:19
Proverbs 12:25
Ecclesiastes 11:10
Isaiah 41:10
1 Peter 5:7

ARGUMENTS
Proverbs 15:1-9
Proverbs 26:17-28
Isaiah 59:4
Philippians 2:12-18
Colossians 2:4
2 Timothy 2:23
Titus 3:1-11

ARROGANCE
1 Samuel 2:3
1 Samuel 15:23
Psalm 10:2
Proverbs 8:13
Isaiah 9:9
Mark 7:22
2 Corinthians 12:20

ASHAMED
2 Samuel 19:3
Psalm 83:17
Isaiah 41:11
Ezekiel 43:10
Luke 9:26

ASSOCIATIONS—GOOD/BAD
Proverbs 9:6

Proverbs 13:20
Proverbs 14:9
Proverbs 22:24-25
Proverbs 23:20-21
Proverbs 29:24
Romans 16:17-18
1 Corinthians 5:9-13
2 Corinthians 6:14-18
2 Timothy 3:5

ASSURANCE
1 Timothy 3:13
Hebrews 4:16
Hebrews 6:11
Hebrews 10:22
Hebrews 11:1
1 Peter 1:3-5
2 Peter 1:10
1 John 5:13, 18-19

ASTRAY
Proverbs 5:23
Proverbs 10:17
Proverbs 12:26
Proverbs 20:1
Isaiah 53:6
1 John 3:7

ATTENTION
Exodus 15:26
Deuteronomy 7:12
Proverbs 4:1
Proverbs 5:1
Proverbs 22:17

ATTITUDE
1 Kings 11:11

Daniel 3:19
Romans 15:5
Ephesians 4:23
Philippians 2:5-11
Philippians 4:4-9
Hebrews 4:12
1 Peter 4:1

AUTHORITY FIGURES
Matthew 22:21
Romans 13:1-7
Ephesians 5:21
1 Timothy 2:1-4
Titus 3:1
1 Peter 2:13-19

AVOIDANCE
Genesis 3:8
Proverbs 14:34
Proverbs 18:1
1 Timothy 6:6-21
2 Timothy 2:22-26

BACKSLIDING
Deuteronomy 8:10-20
Jeremiah 2:19
Jeremiah 3:22
Jeremiah 15:6
Ezekiel 37:23
Luke 9:57-62
James 5:15-20

BAPTISIM
Matthew 28:19
Luke 3:3
Romans 6:4
Ephesians 4:5

Colossians 2:12
1 Peter 3:21

BELIEF
Genesis
John 1:12
John 3:16
Romans 10:5-13
2 Thessalonians 2:13
Hebrews 3:12
James 2:14-26

BEREAVEMENT
Deuteronomy 31:8
Psalm 23:1-6
Psalm 27:10
Psalm 119:50
2 Corinthians 1:3-5
Hebrews 13:5

BITTERNESS
Proverbs 14:10
Proverbs 26:26
Ephesians 4:31
Colossians 3:8
Hebrews 12:14-17
1 John 3:11-24

BLAMELESSNESS
Psalm 1:1-2
Psalm 37:37
Psalm 112:6
Proverbs 11:4
Proverbs 16:8, 11
Proverbs 19:1
Proverbs 21:1, 3
Proverbs 26:6, 13

BLAME SHIFTING
Genesis 3:1-13
1 Samuel 15:10-23
Proverbs 19:3
Galatians 6:5-8
James 4:1-4

BODY
Romans 12:1-2
1 Corinthians 3:16-17
1 Corinthians 6:18-20
2 Corinthians 5:1-4
1 Thessalonians 4:2-8

BORROWING
Exodus 22:14
Deuteronomy 15:6
Psalm 37:21, 25
Proverbs 3:27-28
Proverbs 14:31
Proverbs 22:7

BROKEN SPIRIT
Psalm 34:18
Psalm 51:17
Proverbs 15:13
Proverbs 17:22
Proverbs 18:14

BUDGETING
Proverbs 16:9
Proverbs 19:21
Proverbs 22:3
Proverbs 24:3-4
Proverbs 27:12
Luke 14:28-30
1 Corinthians 16:1-2

BURDEN
Psalm 68:19
Matthew 11:30
Luke 11:46
Galatians 6:2
1 John 5:3

BUSYBODIES
1 Thessalonians 4:11
1 Thessalonians 5:14
2 Thessalonians 3:6
2 Thessalonians 3:11
1 Timothy 5:13
1 Peter 4:15

CARES
Psalm 37:5
Psalm 55:22
Psalm 56:3-4
Proverbs 12:10
Nahum 1:7
Matthew 6:25, 34
Philippians 4:6
Hebrews 13:5-6
1 Peter 5:7

CAUTION
Proverbs 8:12
Proverbs 12:16, 23
Proverbs 13:16
Proverbs 14:8, 15, 18
Proverbs 16:21
Proverbs 18:15
Proverbs 23:3
Proverbs 27:12

CHANGE
Ezekiel 36:25-27
Matthew 16:24
Ephesians 4:17-32
Colossians 3:1-14
1 Thessalonians 1:9
2 Timothy 3:17
Hebrews 10:25
James 1:14-15
1 Peter 3:9

CHARACTER
Psalm 26:4
Psalm 141:4
Proverbs 4:14
Proverbs 12:4
Proverbs 31:10
Acts 17:11
Romans 5:1-5
1 Corinthians 15:33
Galatians 6:7
James 1:22

CHILDREN
Exodus 20:12
Proverbs 1:8
Proverbs 6:20
Proverbs 23:22
Ephesians 6:1
Colossians 3:20-25

CHOICES
Joshua 24:15
1 Chronicles 28:9
Proverbs 1:1-19
Proverbs 3:5-6
Proverbs 8:10

Proverbs 13:1-16
Proverbs 16:3
Psalm 119:30
Psalm 119:111-112
Proverbs 8:10
Proverbs 16:16
Matthew 6:24
Matthew 9:9-13
John 15:16
Romans 6:16
Colossians 3:17, 23
Revelation 3:15

CHURCH
Matthew 18:15-17
Acts 16:5
Acts 20:28
Ephesians 4:1-16
1 Timothy 3:15-16
Hebrews 10:25
Revelation 2, 3

COMFORT
Psalm 23
Psalm 119:50, 52
Isaiah 40:1
Isaiah 49:13
Lamentations 3:21-26
2 Corinthians 1:3-7

COMPLAINING
Numbers 14:27
Psalm 142:2
John 6:43
Philippians 2:3
Philippians 2:12-18
James 5:9

1 Peter 4:9
Jude 16

COMMANDMENT
Exodus 20
Deuteronomy 6:6
Proverbs 13:13
John 13:34
John 15:12
1 John 5:2-3

COMMUNICATION
Psalm 52:2
Psalm 73:7-9
Matthew 12:34-37
Ephesians 4:25-32
Colossians 3:8-9
Colossians 4:6
James 3:2-8

CONFESSION
Isaiah 59:1
Proverbs 28:13
1 Timothy 6:12
James 5:16
1 John 1:9

CONFIDENCE
Psalm 71:5
Proverbs 3:32
Proverbs 11:13
Isaiah 32:17
Jeremiah 17:7

CONFLICTS
Proverbs 10:12
Proverbs 15:1, 18
Proverbs 16:28

Proverbs 28:25
Proverbs 29:22
Galatians 5:17
James 4:1-12

CONFORMITY
Exodus 23:2
John 7:7
Romans 12:1-2
1 Corinthians 3:19
2 Corinthians 4:4
2 Corinthians 6:14-17
Ephesians 4:17-20
James 4:4
1 Peter 1:14
2 Peter 1:4
1 John 2:15-17

CONSCIENCE
Proverbs 28:13-18
Acts 23:1
Acts 24:16
Romans 2:15
1 Corinthians 8:10-12
1 Timothy 1:5, 19
1 Timothy 3:8-9
2 Timothy 1:3
Hebrews 10:21-22
Hebrews 13:18
1 Peter 3:16, 21

CONTEMPT
Job 12:5
Proverbs 14:31
Proverbs 17:5
Proverbs 18:3
Proverbs 19:16

CONTENTMENT
Proverbs 30:7-9
Matthew 20:1-16
2 Corinthians 6:10
Philippians 4:11-12
Colossians 3:2
1 Thessalonians 5:16-18
1 Timothy 6:6-10
Hebrews 13:5

CONVICTION
Proverbs 24:5
John 16:7-11
1 Thessalonians 1:5
2 Timothy 3:17
Hebrews 3:14
James 2:9

CORRUPTION
Isaiah 1:4
Mark 8:36-37
Galatians 6:8
James 4:1-4
1 Peter 4:2-3
2 Peter 1:4
2 Peter 2:18-20
1 John 2:15-16

COUNSEL
Proverbs 3:13
Proverbs 12:5, 12
Proverbs 13:20
Proverbs 14:7
Proverbs 15:22
Proverbs 19:20
Proverbs 24:3, 6
Proverbs 27:9

COSIGNING NOTES
Proverbs 6:1-5
Proverbs 11:15
Proverbs 17:18
Proverbs 20:16
Proverbs 22:20
Proverbs 27:13

COURAGE
Deuteronomy 31:6-9
Joshua 1:5-9
1 Chronicles 22:13
Psalm 27:14
Isaiah 43:1-5
Jeremiah 1:8
Ephesians 6:10
2 Corinthians 12:9-10
2 Timothy 2:1

CRAFTY
Genesis 3:1
Job 5:12-13
Proverbs 7:10
Proverbs 12:2
Proverbs 14:17
1 Corinthians 3:19
Ephesians 4:14

CRITICISM
Proverbs 15:13
Matthew 7:1-5
Luke 6:37
Luke 17:1-4
Romans 2:1-2
Romans 14
Galatians 5:13-26
James 3:1

James 4:11-12

COUNSELING
Job 12:13
Psalm 16:7
Psalm 32:8
Psalm 33:8
Psalm 119:24
Proverbs 11:14
Proverbs 15:22
Proverbs 24:6
Isaiah 11:2

CURSES
Genesis 3:14
Leviticus 20:9
Proverbs 20:20
Proverbs 28:27
Romans 3:14
James 3:10

DEATH
Psalm 23:6
Proverbs 3:21-26
Proverbs 10:16
Proverbs 11:4
Proverbs 14:32
Romans 5:17
Romans 8:10
Romans 14:7-9
1 Corinthians 15:54-58
Philippians 1:21, 23
Hebrews 2:9-10, 14-15

DECEIT
Psalm 17:1
Psalm 26:4
Psalm 32:2
Psalm 52:2
Psalm 119:29
Proverbs 12:5
1 Peter 2

DECISION-MAKING
Psalm 37:3, 5
Psalm 62:8
Proverbs 3:5-6
Isaiah 26:3-4
Isaiah 28:7
Jeremiah 17:7-8
2 Timothy 3:15-17
Hebrews 11:23-27

DEPRAVITY
Proverbs 1:7, 29
Jeremiah 9:6
Hosea 4:6
Romans 1:18, 21, 28
Romans 8:7-8
2 Corinthians 4:4-6
Philippians 2:15
2 Thessalonians 2:10-12
2 Timothy 3:8
2 Peter 2:2

DEPRESSION
Genesis 4:6-7
1 Kings 19:1-9
Psalm 32
Psalm 38
Psalm 42:1-11
Psalm 51
Proverbs 18:14
2 Corinthians 4:8-9

DESIRES
Genesis 3:6
Exodus 20:17
Proverbs 10:3, 24
Proverbs 11:6
Proverbs 28:25
Matthew 6:21
Luke 12:31-34
Galatians 5:16-17
Ephesians 2:3
Titus 2:12
Titus 3:3
James 1:13-16
James 4:1-3
1 Peter 1:14
1 Peter 4:2-3
1 John 2:16
Jude 18

DESPAIR
Exodus 14:1-17
Psalm 25:17
Psalm 40:1-17
Psalm 62:2
Psalm 73:26
Psalm 88:15
Proverbs 24:16
Ecclesiastes 2:20
Isaiah 40:31
John 14:1
2 Corinthians 1:8-10
2 Corinthians 4:8
2 Corinthians 6:4
Hebrews 12:5

DIFFICULTIES
Romans 8:28, 35-39
2 Corinthians 1:4
2 Corinthians 4:17
2 Corinthians 12:10
Hebrews 12:7-11
James 1:2
1 Peter 1:6-7
Revelation 3:19

DILIGENCE
Proverbs 6:4
Proverbs 12:11, 24
Proverbs 13:4, 11
Proverbs 16:3
Proverbs 21:5
Proverbs 24:2-4, 7
1 Thessalonians 4:11
2 Timothy 2:6

DISAPPOINTMENT
Psalm 31:14
Psalm 42:5, 11
Psalm 43:5
Psalm 55:22
Psalm 62:5
Psalm 71:14
Psalm 126:6
John 14:1, 27
2 Corinthians 4:8-10

DISCOURAGEMENT
Joshua 1:9
Psalm 27:14
Psalm 119:28

Isaiah 61:3
Matthew 11:28
Colossians 1:5
Hebrews 12:11
James 4:9
1 Peter 1:3-9
1 John 5:14

DISCERNMENT
Exodus 18:21
Leviticus 19:15
2 Chronicles 19:5-10
Psalm 119:36, 125
Proverbs 28:2
Ecclesiastes 12:13
Matthew 7:1-12
James 1:2-8

DISCIPLINE
Proverbs 3:11-12
Proverbs 13:24
Proverbs 19:18
Proverbs 22:6, 15
Proverbs 23:13
Proverbs 29:15
1 Corinthians 5:1-13
1 Corinthians 11:29-34
2 Corinthians 2:1-11
Ephesians 6:1-4
1 Timothy 4:7
Hebrews 12:7-11

DISCOURAGEMENT
Deuteronomy 1:21
Joshua 1:9
2 Chronicles 20:17

Psalm 46:11
Isaiah 41:10
Amos 5:14
Romans 8:31
2 Timothy 4:22

DISHONESTY
Exodus 18:21
Leviticus 19:35
Deuteronomy 25:16
Proverbs 13:11
Proverbs 20:23-26
Proverbs 29:27
Luke 16:8-10
1 Timothy 3:8
Titus 1:7, 11
1 Peter 5:2

DISOBEDIENCE
Genesis 3:1-24
1 Chronicles 13:1-14
Romans 5:17-21
Ephesians 4:29
2 Timothy 2:15
Hebrews 4:1, 11
Hebrews 12:15
2 Peter 1:10-11

DIVISIONS
Proverbs 10:12
Romans 13:13
1 Corinthians 1:10
1 Corinthians 4:6-13
2 Corinthians 12:20
Galatians 5:20
James 4:1-3

DIVORCE AND REMARRIAGE
Genesis 2:24
Deuteronomy 24:1-4
Isaiah 50:1
Jeremiah 3:1
Malachi 2:15-16
Matthew 5:31-32
Matthew 19:3-9
Mark 10:3-5
1 Corinthians 7:10-24, 33-40

DOUBLE-MINDEDNESS
2 Kings 17:41
Isaiah 29:13
Psalm 119:113
Matthew 6:24
James 1:8
James 4:8
2 Peter 3:16

DOUBTFUL THINGS
Romans 14:1-23
1 Corinthians 8:9, 13
Philippians 2:15
Colossians 3:2, 5-20, 17
1 Thessalonians 5:22
Titus 2:12-14
1 Peter 5:7
1 John 2:15-17

DUTY
Deuteronomy 6:2
Deuteronomy 10:12
Psalm 111:10
Proverbs 1:7

Ecclesiastes 12:13
Romans 13:7-9
1 Peter 2:17
Revelation 19:5

DRINKING
Proverbs 20:1
Proverbs 23:20, 29-35
Proverbs 31:4-6
Isaiah 5:22
Luke 12:45
Luke 21:34
1 Corinthians 5:11
1 Corinthians 6:10
Galatians 5:21
Ephesians 5:15-20

EGO
Psalm 75:4
Proverbs 11:12
Proverbs 12:9
Proverbs 15:25
Proverbs 16:18-19
Proverbs 18:12, 23
Proverbs 29:23
Matthew 23:12
Philippians 2:3

ENCOURAGEMENT
Joshua 1:9
Acts 20:2
Romans 12:8
Romans 15:4-5
Philippians 2:1
1 Thessalonians 5:1-28
2 Thessalonians 2:16

1 Peter 1:1-13

ENTHUSIASM
Ecclesiastes 9:10
2 Corinthians 9:2
Ephesians 6:7
Colossians 3:18-25
1 Peter 2:15
1 Peter 4:11

ENVY
Deuteronomy 5:21
1 Kings 2l: 1-29
1 Corinthians 3:3
Galatians 5:20
Titus 3:3
James 3:14-16
1 Peter 2:1

ETERNAL LIFE
Luke 18:18-30
John 3:1-21, 36
John 6:40, 60-71
John 10:28
John 17:1-26
Romans 5:21
Romans 6:23
1 Timothy 1:6
Titus 1:2
1 John 2:25
1 John 5:1-13
Jude 21

EVIL
Genesis 2:9, 15-17
Genesis 6:5

Psalm 97:10
Proverbs 8:13
Isaiah 5:20
Amos 5:15
Matthew 6:13
Romans 12:9
1 Thessalonians 5:22
2 Timothy 2:19

EVILDOOER
2 Samuel 3:39
Psalm 26:5
Psalm 94:4
Psalm 101:8
Proverbs 4:14
Proverbs 12:13
Proverbs 21:15

EXCELLENCE
Proverbs 18:9
Proverbs 22:20
Philippians 4:8
Colossians 3:17, 23
1 Peter 4:11
Titus 3:8

FAITH
Psalm 14:2
Habakkuk 2:4
Romans 1:16-17
Romans 3:28
1 Timothy 1:5
Hebrews 10:39
Hebrews 11:6
James 1:6
James 2:18

FAITHLESS
Psalm 101:3
Proverbs 14:14
Jeremiah 3:22
Mark 8:38
Romans 2:3
2 Timothy 2:13
Hebrews 4:1
2 Peter 2:1

FALSE DOCTRINE
Proverbs 4:2
Romans 16:17-18
1 Timothy 1:10
1 Timothy 4:1-16
1 Timothy 6:1-5
2 Timothy 4:3
Titus 2:1, 7-10
2 John 9

FALSEHOOD
Leviticus 19:11
Psalm 52:3
Psalm 119:25
Proverbs 12:19, 22
Proverbs 30:8
Ephesians 4:25
Colossians 3:9
Revelation 21:8
Revelation 22:15

FAMILY
Genesis 2:18, 24
Genesis 7:1
Exodus 20:12
Proverbs 14:26
Ephesians 5:25, 31

1 Corinthians 13:1-13
1 Peter 3:7

FAULTS
Job 22:5
Job 34:32
Psalm 19:12
Psalm 51:2
Isaiah 64:6
Matthew 7:1-5
Romans 7:14-25
1 Corinthians 4:4
Ephesians 4:1-16
James 5:16
1 John 1:9

FEAR
Genesis 3:10
Joshua 1:1-18
Psalm 27:1
Psalm 56:11
Psalm 91:1-6
Psalm 121:1-8
Proverbs 29:25
Matthew 10:26-31
2 Timothy 1:7
Hebrews 2:14-15
1 Peter 3:6, 13-14
1 John 4:18

FEELINGS
Proverbs 12:16, 23
Proverbs 14:33
Proverbs 15:28
Proverbs 29:11, 20
Amos 5:13
Romans 7:14-25

1 Corinthians 13:1-13

FIGHT
Exodus 14:14
Deuteronomy 1:30
Deuteronomy 3:22
1 Corinthians 10:3-4
Ephesians 6:12-18
1 Timothy 1:18
1 Timothy 6:12
2 Timothy 2:3-5
2 Timothy 4:7

FLESH
Job 14:4
Matthew 15:19
Mark 7:21
Romans 1:28
Romans 7:18-23
Romans 8:5-17
Ephesians 2:3
Ephesians 4:18
Colossians 1:21
2 Thessalonians 2:12

FOOLISHNESS
Psalm 14:1-7
Proverbs 9:1-18
1 Corinthians 1:18-25
1 Corinthians 2:6-16
1 Corinthians 3:19

FORGIVENESS
Psalm 51:1-19
Proverbs 17:9
Matthew 6:5-15
Matthew 18:15-17, 21-35

Mark 11:25
Luke 17:3
Romans 12:1-21
Ephesians 4:32
Colossians 3:13
James 5:15
1 John 1:1-10

FRIENDSHIP
Proverbs 17:1-28
Proverbs 27:6, 10
Matthew 6:24
John 15:1-17
2 Corinthians 6:14
James 4:4

FRUIT OF THE SPIRIT
Matthew 12:33
John 15:5, 16
Romans 6:22
Romans 7:4
Galatians 5:16-18, 22-26
Ephesians 5:9
Philippians 1:11
Colossians 1:10

FUTURE
Joshua 4:21
Psalm 37:37-38
Psalm 102:18
Proverbs 24:14
Jeremiah 29:11
Revelation 21:1-4

GAMBLING
Proverbs 15:16
Proverbs 23:4-5

Matthew 16:25-26
Luke 12:15
1 Corinthians 6:12
1 Corinthians 10:31
Colossians 3:2, 5-6
1 Timothy 6:9

GENTLENESS
2 Corinthians 10:1
Galatians 5:23
Philippians 4:5
Colossians 3:12
1 Timothy 6:1
2 Timothy 2:14-16
James 3:1-18
1 Peter 3:15

GIFTS
John 15:26
Romans 12:3-8
1 Corinthians 12-14
Ephesians 1:5
Ephesians 4:8-11
1 Peter 4:10:11
Hebrews 2:4

GIVING
Exodus 25:2
Proverbs 11:25
Proverbs 22:9
Luke 6:38
Acts 20:35
Romans 12:8
2 Corinthians 8:12
2 Corinthians 9:7
James 1:17-18

GODLINESS
1 Timothy 2:2
1 Timothy 4:8
1 Timothy 6:5-6, 11
2 Timothy 3:5
Titus 1:1
2 Peter 1:6-7

GOODNESS
Psalm 23:6
Micah 6:8
Matthew 7:17-18
Matthew 12:33-35
Romans 8:28
Galatians 5:22
Ephesians5:9
Philippians 4:8
2 Peter 1:5

GOSSIP
Exodus 23:1-9
Proverbs 10:18
Proverbs 11:13
Proverbs 18:8
Proverbs 20:19
Proverbs 25:18-28
Proverbs 26:20-22
James 4:11

GRATITUDE
Psalm 92:1-5
Psalm 136:1-6, 23-26
Ephesians 5:4, 20
Philippians 4:6
Colossians 3:15, 17
1 Thessalonians 5:18

GREED
Proverbs 15:27
Proverbs 28:25
Proverbs 29:4
Jeremiah 6:13
Matthew 23:25
Mark 7:21-22
Luke 12:15
Romans 1:29
Ephesians 4:19
Colossians 3:5
James 4:1-17

GRIEF
Psalm 34:18
Proverbs 14:13
Proverbs 15:13
Matthew 11:28-30
Ephesians 4:30
Philippians 4:13
1 Thessalonians 4:13-18
Revelation 21:4

GRUMBLING
Exodus 16:7-8
Psalm 106:25
1 Corinthians 10:10
Philippians 2:14
James 5:9
1 Peter 4:9
Jude 16

GUIDANCE
Psalm 25:5
Proverbs 1:5
Proverbs 3:5-6
Proverbs 4:11

Proverbs 6:22
Proverbs 11:14
Proverbs 20:18
Proverbs 24:6

GUILT
Psalm 32:1-2
Isaiah 1:18
Isaiah 43:25
Acts 3:19
Romans 8:1-17
Colossians 2:9-17
1 John 3:11-24

HABITS
Proverbs 19:19
Jeremiah 22:21
Romans 6-7
1 Corinthians 15:33
Galatians 5:16-21
1 Timothy 5:13
Hebrews 10:25
1 John 3:1-24

HAPPINESS
Psalm 37:4
Psalm 68:3
Proverbs 15:13
Ecclesiastes 5:19
Matthew 5:1-12
Matthew 25:21-23
1 Timothy 6:3-10
James 5:13

HATE
Leviticus 19:17
Psalm 5:5

Proverbs 6:16-19
Proverbs 8:13
Proverbs 9:8
Proverbs 26:28
Luke 6:22,27
1 John 2:9
1 John 4:20

HEAVEN
Isaiah 65:17
John 14:1-14
2 Corinthians 5:1
Colossians 3:1-17
Hebrews 8:1
2 Peter 3:13
Revelation 21:1-2

HELL
Matthew 5:22, 29-30
Matthew 10:28
Matthew 18:9
Matthew 25:41-46
Luke 12:5
James 3:6
2 Peter 2:4
Revelation 20:1-15

HELP
Psalm 28:7
Psalm 46:1-11
Psalm 54:4
1 Corinthians 12:28
Galatians 6:1-10
1 Timothy 5:10
Hebrews 13:6

HOARDING
Psalm 49:11, 16-17
Proverbs 13:22
Proverbs 28:22
Malachi 3:8
Matthew 6:24
Luke 12:21, 33

HOLINESS
Exodus 15:11
1 Chronicles 16:29
Psalm 29:2
Isaiah 35:8
1 Corinthians 1:30
Ephesians 4:24
Hebrews 12:14
1 Peter 1:16:8-11

HOMOSEXUALITY
Genesis 2:24
Genesis 9:7
Genesis 19
Leviticus 18:22
Leviticus 20:13
Romans 1:24-32
Romans 12:1-2
1 Corinthians 6:9-11
Ephesians 4:22-24
1 Timothy 1:8-11

HONESTY
Deuteronomy 25:15
Proverbs 6:16-20
Proverbs 11:3
Proverbs 12:17, 22

Proverbs 14:5
Proverbs 16:13
Proverbs 24:26
Colossians 3:9
Hebrews 13:18

HOPE
Job 13:15
Job 27:8
Psalm 25:3
Proverbs 10:28
Proverbs 13:12
Romans 5:1-11
1 Thessalonians 1:3
1 Thessalonians 4:13-18
Hebrews 6:11

HOT-TEMPEREDNESS
Proverbs 10:12
Proverbs 15:18
Proverbs 19:19
Proverbs 22:24
Proverbs 26:21
Proverbs 29:22
James 3:14-16

HOTHEADEDNESS
Numbers 22:27
Proverbs 12:15
Proverbs 14:16
Proverbs 15:21
Proverbs 18:6
Proverbs 28:14
Proverbs 29:9
Matthew 5:22
Mark 6:17-19
John 9:40

HUMILITY
Proverbs 3:34
Proverbs 15:33
Proverbs 16:19
Proverbs 22:4
Proverbs 29:23
Jeremiah 9:23-24
Galatians 6:1-2
Philippians 2:1-11
James 4:6, 10
1 Peter 5:6-7

HURT
Psalm 55:22
Psalm 56:3-4
Psalm 121:1-8
Luke 6:27
Acts 7:26
1 Peter 5:7
Revelation 2:11

HUSBANDS AND WIVES
Genesis 2:18, 24
Ephesians 5:22-33
Colossians 3:18-21
1 Timothy 2:11-15
Titus 2:4-5
1 Peter 3:1-17

IMMORALITY
Matthew 5:32
Matthew 15:19
Mark 7:21
Acts 15:20
Romans 13:13
1 Corinthians 6:1-20
Galatians 5:19

Ephesians 5:3
Colossians 3:5
1 Thessalonians 4:3
Revelation 9:13-21

INDECISIVENESS
Joshua 24:15
2 Chronicles 13:7
Ecclesiastes 11:9
Matthew 6:24
Luke 14:25-33
John 3:22-36

IDENTITY
Ezekiel 36:26-27
John 1:12
Romans 8:15-16
Romans 15:7
1 Corinthians 2:16
2 Corinthians 5:17-21
Ephesians 1:4-5
Colossians 1:22
Colossians 2:9-11
Hebrews 10:14
1 Peter 1:23

INFERIORITY
Psalm 86:13
Psalm 139:13-16
Matthew 5:3
1 Corinthians 1:26-29
Colossians 3:10
1 Peter 2:9-10

INSPIRATION
Deuteronomy 7:9
Psalm 25:10

Romans 15:4
1 Thessalonians 1:3
2 Timothy 3:16
Hebrews 12:14

INSULT
1 Samuel 25:14
Psalm 22:7
Proverbs 9:7
Proverbs 12:16
Proverbs 22:10
Isaiah 51:7
Matthew 5:11
Matthew 27:39, 44
Luke 6:22
1 Peter 3:9

INTEGRITY
1 Kings 9:4
1 Chronicles 29:17
Job 2:3, 9
Psalm 25:1-21
Psalm 41:12
Proverbs 10:9
Proverbs 11:3
Proverbs 13:6
Matthew 22:16
Luke 16:1-15
Titus 2:7

JEALOUSY
Exodus 34:14
Proverbs 6:34
Proverbs 27:4
Acts 5:17
Romans 13:3
1 Corinthians 3:3

2 Corinthians 12:20
Galatians 5:19-21

JESUS
Luke 2:11
John 3:16
Acts 2:36
Acts 4:12
Acts 10:36
Romans 5:11
Romans 6:23
Romans 8:39
1 Timothy 1:15
1 Peter 3:18

JOY
Psalm 28:7
Psalm 33:1
Psalm 66:1
Psalm 81:1
Psalm 100:2
Romans 12:12
Romans 14:17
Galatians 5:22
James 1:2

JUDGING
Proverbs 24:23
Matthew 7:1-5
Luke 6:37
John 7:24
Romans 2:1-2
Romans 14:10-13
1 Corinthians 5:1-13
James 3:1
James 4:11-12

KINDNESS
Psalm 86:5
Luke 6:27-36
Acts 28:2
Romans 12:10
1 Corinthians 13:4
Galatians 5:22
Ephesians 4:32
Colossians 3:1-17
1 Peter 1:2-11

LAZINESS
Proverbs 12:24, 27
Proverbs 13:4
Proverbs 15:19
Proverbs 18:9
Proverbs 26:13-16
Matthew 25:26
2 Thessalonians 3:6-15
2 Peter 3:1-18

LENDING
Exodus 22:25-26
Deuteronomy 24:10-11
Psalm 15:5
Psalm 37:26
Luke 6:34-35
Luke 7:41

LIFE-DOMINATING PROBLEMS
Proverbs 5:1-23
1 Corinthians 6:9-12
Galatians 5:16-21
Ephesians 5:18
1 Thessalonians 4:1-8
Revelation 21:8

Revelation 22:15

LIFESTYLE
Matthew 5:1-12
Luke 6:31
1 Corinthians 9:1-27
1 Corinthians 13
Galatians 5:22-26
Colossians 3:17
2 Timothy 2:14-16
James 1:2-8

LISTENING
Proverbs 5:1-2
Proverbs 13:18
Proverbs 15:31
Proverbs 18:13
Proverbs 19:27
Proverbs 25:12
James 1:19

LONELINESS
Psalm 23:1-6
Psalm 25:16
Isaiah 41:10
Matthew 28:20
John 14:16, 18
Hebrews 13:5-6

LORD'S PRAYER
Matthew 6:9-13
John 17:1-26

LOVE
Deuteronomy 6:5
Proverbs 10:12
Proverbs 17:19
Matthew 5:44

Matthew 22:39-40
John 3:16
John 13:34-35
Romans 13:10
1 Corinthians 13
1 John 4:10, 19
1 John 5:2-3
2 John 5, 6

LUST
Job 31:1
Proverbs 6:25
Matthew 5:28
Mark 7:20-23
Romans 1:26
Romans 6:12
1 Thessalonians 4:3-8
James 1:14-15
1 John 2:16

LYING
Exodus 20:16
Proverbs 12:19, 22
Proverbs 17:20
Proverbs 19:9
Proverbs 24:24
Proverbs 26:28
Proverbs 29:12
Matthew 5:37
Ephesians 4:17-32
Colossians 3:9

MALICE
Mark 7:18-23
Romans 1:29
1 Corinthians 5:8
Ephesians 4:31

Colossians 3:8
Titus 3:3
1 Peter 2:1

MARRIAGE
Genesis 1:27
Genesis 2:21-24
Matthew 19:4-6
1 Corinthians 7:1-4
Ephesians 5:28
Hebrews 13:4

MATERIALISM
Psalm 39:6
Psalm 62:10
Proverbs 11:4
Proverbs 16:16
Proverbs 23:5
Ecclesiastes 2:26
Ecclesiastes 5:10
Matthew 6:19-24
1 Timothy 6:8-10
Hebrews 13:5
1 John 2:15-17

MERCY
Psalm 4:1
Psalm 25:6-7
Psalm 57:1
Psalm 59:16
Psalm 86:3-5
Habakkuk 3:2
John 3:16-17

MOCKER
Psalm 1:1-3
Proverbs 3:34

Proverbs 9:7-8, 12
Proverbs 14:6
Proverbs 15:2
Proverbs 20:1
Proverbs 21:24
Proverbs 22:10

MONEY
Deuteronomy 8:18
Psalm 62:10
Proverbs 10:22
Proverbs 11:28
Proverbs 23:5
Ecclesiastes 5:19
1 Corinthians 16:2
1 Timothy 6:10

MORALITY
Psalm 86:11
Romans 2:1-16
Romans 6:11
Romans 12:1-8
Romans 13:13
1 Corinthians 15:33
Colossians 3:17

MOTIVES
Jeremiah 17:1-18
Proverbs 16:2
1 Corinthians 4:5
Philippians 1:18
1 Thessalonians 2:3
James 4:1-12

MOTHERS
Genesis 3:20
Proverbs 1:8

Proverbs 23:22
Proverbs 30:11
Proverbs 31:26-27
Ephesians 6:1

MURDER
Numbers 35:30-31
Deuteronomy 5:1-33
1 Timothy 1:9
James 4:1-12
Revelation 21:8
Revelation 22:15

NEEDS
Psalm 37:25
Proverbs 12:10
Isaiah 58:11
Matthew 6:8, 25-33
2 Corinthians 9:12
Ephesians 4:29
Philippians 4:19
James 2:14-16

NEIGHBOR
Proverbs 3:28-29
Proverbs 14:21
Proverbs 26:18-20
Romans 13:10
1 John 2:9-10
1 John 4:20-21

NEW PERSON
Psalm 51:10
Ezekiel 36:26
Ezekiel 51:10
John 3:3
Ephesians 2:10

Ephesians 4:22-24
2 Corinthians 5:17

OBEDIENCE
Deuteronomy 30:11-19
1 Samuel 15:22
Luke 17:9-10
Acts 4:19
Acts 5:29
Romans 5:1-21
Ephesians 6:1
Hebrews 5:8
Hebrews 13:17
1 Peter 1:22

OCCULT
Deuteronomy 18:9-13
1 Samuel 28:7-12
2 Kings 21:6
Isaiah 47:13-14
Acts 19:18-20

OLD AGE
Leviticus 19:32
Isaiah 46:4
Psalm 48:14
Psalm 71:6, 9, 14
Proverbs 17:6

OPPRESSION
Psalm 9:9
Psalm 72:14
Psalm 82:3
Psalm 103:6
Psalm 119:34
Psalm 146:7
Zechariah 7:10

PARTIALITY
Leviticus 19:15
Deuteronomy 1:17
Deuteronomy 10:17
Proverbs 24:23
1 Timothy 5:21
James 2:1-13

PATIENCE
Psalm 37:5-7
Proverbs 14:29-30
Proverbs 19:11
Proverbs 25:15
Ecclesiastes 7:8
Colossians 1:11
1 Timothy 1:16
2 Timothy 4:2
Hebrews 12:1-3
James 5:7-8

PAIN
Job 6:10
Psalm 6:6
Psalm 38:17
Psalm 69:26
Isaiah 53:3-5
Hebrews 12:1-13
Revelation 21:4

PEACE
Psalm 3:1-8
Proverbs 3:1-2
Proverbs 16:7
John 14:1-31
Romans 5:1-11
Romans 12:18

Romans 14:19
Philippians 4:6-9
Colossians 3:15
Hebrews 12:14

PERSEVERANCE
Romans 5:3-4
Romans 15:5
Hebrews 12:1
James 1:3-5
James 5:11
2 Peter 1:6

PERVERSION
Leviticus 18:23
Leviticus 20:12
Romans 1:26-27
1 Corinthians 6:9
2 Peter 2:1-22
Jude 7

PORNOGRAPHY
Romans 6:12
Romans 8:6,13
1 Corinthians 6:9, 13, 18
Galatians 5:17
James 1:15

POVERTY
Exodus 23:6
Deuteronomy 15:7-8
Proverbs 10:4, 15
Proverbs 13:18
Proverbs 22:16
Proverbs 14:23
Proverbs 30:8
2 Corinthians 8:9

PRAISE
2 Samuel 22:50
Psalm 47:6
Psalm 146:1-10
Psalm 150
Luke 19:37-40
Hebrews 13:15
1 Peter 2:9

PARENT AND CHILD
Genesis 2:24
Psalm 127:3-5
Proverbs 31:26-27
2 Corinthians 12:14
Ephesians 6:1-4
1 Timothy 3:4-5

PRAYER
2 Chronicles 7:14
Jeremiah 29:12
Colossians 4:2
1 Thessalonians 5:16-18
James 5:13
1 John 5:14-16

PREJUDICE
Genesis 1:27
Proverbs 26:12
Matthew 7:1-4
Romans 2:11
Romans 15:7
1 Corinthians 13
Galatians 3:28
Colossians 3:13
James 2:1
2 Peter 1:3-4

1 John 2:9-11

PRIDE
Proverbs 8:13
Proverbs 11:2
Proverbs 13:10
Proverbs 16:18
Proverbs 18:12
Proverbs 21:24
Proverbs 27:1
Proverbs 29:23

PRIORITIES
2 Chronicles 31:20
Proverbs 2:1-9
Proverbs 3:1-35
Matthew 6:25-34
Luke 12:31
John 6:27
Romans 14:17

PROBLEMS
Romans 5:1-5
Romans 8:35-39
2 Corinthians 1:3-7
2 Corinthians 4:8-10
2 Corinthians 12:10
James 1:1-18
1 Peter 2:6-7

PROCRASTINATION
Psalm 119:60
Proverbs 10:1-32
Proverbs 13:4
Proverbs 26:1-28
Ecclesiastes 5:4
2 Corinthians 6:2

PROVIDENCE
Psalm 145:9, 14-16
Matthew 10:28-31
Matthew 11:28-30
Romans 5:17
Romans 8:28-29, 33-36
1 Corinthians 10:13

QUARRELS
Proverbs 13:1-10
Proverbs 19:13
Proverbs 21:9, 19
Proverbs 22:10
Proverbs 26:21
1 Timothy 3:3
2 Timothy 2:23-24
Titus 3:1-11
James 4:1-12

QUICK-TEMPERED
Proverbs 12:16
Proverbs 14:17, 29
Proverbs 15:18
Proverbs 16:32
Proverbs 22:24
Proverbs 29:22
Titus 1:7

REBELLION
1 Samuel 15:23
Psalm 25:7
Psalm 78:40
Psalm 107:17
Psalm 139:21
Proverbs 17:11
Proverbs 24:21
Proverbs 28:2

REBUKE
Proverbs 9:7-8
Proverbs 13:1
Proverbs 15:31
Proverbs 19:25
Proverbs 27:5
Proverbs 28:3
Proverbs 29:1
1 Timothy 5:20
Hebrews 12:5

RECONCILIATION
Matthew 5:23-24
Matthew 18:15-17
Luke 12:58
Luke 17:3-10
Romans 5:10
Ephesians 2:15-16, 18
1 Corinthians 7:11
2 Corinthians 5:18-20
Colossians 1:19-22

REDEDICATION
Psalm 119:9, 11
Romans 12:1-2
Ephesians 3:16-19
Ephesians 5:15-18
Ephesians 6:18-19
Colossians 3:16-17
1 Thessalonians 5:17
Hebrews 9:14
Hebrews 11:6
James 4:7-8
1 John 1:9

RELATIONSHIPS
Proverbs 18:24

2 Corinthians 6:14-18
Ephesians 2:11-22
Philippians 2:5
James 4:4

REPENTANCE
Joel 2:13-14
Mark 2:16-17
Luke 3:8-14
Luke 24:47
Acts 3:19
Acts 5:31
Acts 17:30
Acts 26:20
2 Corinthians 7:10
2 Corinthians 12:21

RESENTMENT
Job 5:2
Proverbs 26:24-26
Ecclesiastes 7:9
James 1:19-27

RESPECT
Leviticus 19:3, 32
Deuteronomy 1:15
Deuteronomy 10:12-13
Proverbs 13:13
Mark 12:38
Hebrews 12:9, 15
1 Peter 2:17

REVENGE
Leviticus 19:18
Proverbs 6:34
Proverbs 20:22
Matthew 5:43-44

Romans 12:17-21
Ephesians 4:31
Colossians 3:8
1 Peter 2:1

REWARDS AND PUNISHMENT
Proverbs 13:24
Proverbs 22:15
Proverbs 29:15
2 Corinthians 2:6
2 Corinthians 10:6
Hebrews 10:35
Hebrews 11:26
2 John 8

RIGHTEOUSNESS
Genesis 15:6
Psalm 5:8
Psalm 7:17
Psalm 9:8
Psalm 31:1-5
Psalm 51:1-19

SADNESS
Psalm 42:5, 11
Psalm 143:7-8
Matthew 11:28
2 Corinthians 2:4-7
2 Corinthians 7:8-9
Revelation 7:17

SALVATION
Psalm 68:19-20
Luke 9:23-24
John 3:16-17
Romans 10:8-15

Ephesians 2:8-9
Titus 3:3-7

SATAN
Job 1:6-12
Job 2:1-7
Isaiah 14:12-16
Ephesians 6:11-16
James 4:7
1 Peter 5:8-9
1 John 3:8

SCHEMES
Psalm 10:2
Psalm 37:7
Proverbs 6:18-19
Proverbs 10:23
Proverbs 24:9
Ephesians 6:11

SELF
Psalm 139:1-24
Matthew 16:26
Luke 9:25
Romans 6:6
Ephesians 4:24
Colossians 3:10-14

SELF-CENTEREDNESS
Psalm 119:36
Proverbs 18:1
Mark 8:31-38
2 Corinthians 12:20
Galatians 5:20
Philippians 2:3
2 Timothy 3:2-4
James 3:14-16

1 Peter 1:14-25

SELF-CONTROL
Proverbs 16:32
Proverbs 25:28
1 Corinthians 7:5
1 Corinthians 9:25
1 Corinthians 10:13
Galatians 5:22-24
1 Timothy 3:2
Titus 1:8
Titus 2:6, 12
James 1:19-21
2 Peter 2:16

SELF-DENIAL
Matthew 16:24
Mark 10:17-22
Luke 9:23-27
Luke 14:25-27
2 Timothy 3:12
1 Peter 4:1-2

SELFISHNESS
Mark 8:31-38
Luke 6:30-34, 38
Luke 9:23-25
2 Corinthians 9:6-7, 11
Philippians 2:3
James 4:1-10

SELF-IMAGE
Genesis 1:27
1 Samuel 16:7
Psalm 139:14
Ephesians 2:10
Colossians 3:10

SELF-WORTH
Psalm 37:4
Jeremiah 1:5
Jeremiah 29:11
Jeremiah 31:3
Romans 8:28
2 Corinthians 12:9
Philippians 2:13
Philippians 4:13
1 John 3:2-3

SERVICE
Joshua 24:14-22
Mark 10:45
John 13:3-5, 12-17
Romans 12:1, 11
Ephesians 6:7
Colossians 3:17, 23-24

SEX
Genesis 2:25
Proverbs 5:15-21
1 Corinthians 7:1-11
Colossians 1:10
Colossians 3:17
1 Thessalonians 4:1-8

SHAME
Genesis 2:25
Psalm 25:3
Proverbs 11:2
Proverbs 13:18
1 Corinthians 4:14
1 Peter 3:16

SICKNESS
Psalm 41:3
Psalm 103:3
Proverbs 13:12
Proverbs 18:14
Matthew 4:23
John 11:4
James 5:13-15

SIN
Isaiah 53:5-6
Isaiah 59:1-2
John 8:34
Romans 3:23
Romans 6:23
Galatians 6:7-8

SLANDER
Leviticus 19:16
Psalm 5:9
Psalm 55:21
Proverbs 10:18
Proverbs 26:24-26
Ephesians 4:31
Titus 3:2

SORROW
Psalm 31:9
Psalm 34:18
Psalm 90:10
Ecclesiastes 1:18
John 11:33-35
1 Corinthians 7:10
Philippians 2:27
Revelation 21:4

SPEECH
Job 16:3
Proverbs 8:13

Proverbs 12:6
Proverbs 16:24
Matthew 12:34-35

SPIRITUAL GIFTS
Romans 12:4-8
1 Corinthians 12:29-30
Ephesians 4:11-12
1 Peter 4:10-11

STEALING
Exodus 20:15
Proverbs 20:10, 23
Proverbs 29:24
Proverbs 30:7-9
Matthew 6:19-20
Mark 10:19
Ephesians 4:28

STOP
Job 37:14
Isaiah 1:13, 16
John 6:43
John 20:27
1 Corinthians 13:8
1 Corinthians 14:20

STRENGTH
Joshua 1:9
Psalm 119:28
Isaiah 40:29-31
Habakkuk 3:19
2 Corinthians 12:9
Philippians 4:13

STRESS
Psalm 23
Isaiah 49:13

Romans 5:1-5
Romans 13:11-14
2 Corinthians 12:10
Philippians 4:4-9

STUBBORNNESS
1 Samuel 15:23
2 Chronicles 30:8
Psalm 81:12
Jeremiah 5:23
Jeremiah 7:24
Romans 2:5

STUMBLE
Psalm 17:5
Psalm 37:23-25
Psalm 119:165
Proverbs 3:13-26
Proverbs 24:16-17
Isaiah 40:29-31
1 Corinthians 10:32

SUFFERING
Romans 8:18
2 Corinthians 1:5
Philippians 3:10
2 Timothy 2:12
James 1:2-8
1 Peter 1:6-7

SUICIDE
Job 14:5
Psalm 55:4-8
Psalm 139:1-16
Romans 14:7
1 Corinthians 6:19-20
1 Corinthians 10:13

James 4:7

TEMPERENCE
Proverbs 23:20-21
Luke 21:34
Romans 13:13
1 Corinthians 9:25-27
1 Timothy 3:8
Titus 1:7-8
1 Peter 4:3

TEMPTATION
Psalm 94:17-18
Proverbs 28:13
Matthew 6:13
1 Corinthians 10:12-13
Hebrews 4:14-16
James 1:2-14

TEN COMMANDMENTS
Exodus 20:3-17

TEST
Genesis 22:1
Deuteronomy 6:16
Psalm 26:2
1 Thessalonians 5:16-24
Hebrews 3:8
James 1:3
1 John 4:1

TERMINAL ILLNESS
Psalm 139:13-18
Jeremiah 29:11
2 Corinthians 12:9
1 Thessalonians 5:18
2 Timothy 2:12

THANKFULNESS
Psalm 92:1-15
Ephesians 5:20
Colossians 2:7
Colossians 3:15
Colossians 4:2
1 Thessalonians 5:16-18
Hebrews 13:15

TONGUE
Psalm 34:13
Psalm 51:14
Proverbs 10:19
Proverbs 12:18
Proverbs 15:4
Proverbs 21:23
Romans 14:11

TROUBLE
Psalm 9:9
Psalm 34:17
Psalm 41:1
Proverbs 11:8
John 16:33
2 Corinthians 1:3-5
2 Corinthians 4:17

TRUST
Psalm 56:3-4
Proverbs 3:5-6
Isaiah 26:3-4
Jeremiah 29:11
Romans 15:13

TRUSTWORTHINESS
Psalm 19:7
Psalm 111:7

Psalm 119:86
Proverbs 11:13
Proverbs 13:17
Luke 16:10

TRUTH
Psalm 15:2
Psalm 25:2
Proverbs 12:17, 19
Isaiah 65:16
John 1:17
John 4:24
John 8:32
John 14:6
John 16:13

TRUTHFULNESS
Psalm 1:1-2
Proverbs 11:4
Proverbs 19:1
Proverbs 21:3
Romans 13:7, 9
Galatians 6:9

UNBELIEF
Mark 9:24
Romans 4:20
1 Corinthians 7:14
Hebrews 3:12
Revelation 21:8

UNFAITHFUL
Psalm 78:57
Psalm 101:3
Proverbs 11:6
Proverbs 13:2, 15
2 Timothy 2:13

UNPARDONABLE SIN
Matthew 12:31-32
Mark 3:28-29

VALUES
Matthew 6:19-21
Matthew 10:42
Mark 9:36-37
Luke 12:6-7
1 Corinthians 13:1-13
Galatians 5:22-23

VICTORY
Psalm 20:6-9
1 Corinthians 9:24-27
1 Corinthians 15:57
Philippians 2:16
2 Timothy 4:7
Hebrews 12:1
1 John 5:4

WAITING
Psalm 27:1-14
Psalm 40:1-4
Proverbs 8:24
Matthew 24:32-51
Hebrews 6:15
James 5:7

WALK
Psalm 1:1-6
Psalm 15:2
Psalm 16:11
Psalm 17:5
Psalm 119:105
Proverbs 3:5-6
John 14:6

WEAKNESSES
Psalm 31:9-10
Psalm 73:13
Romans 8:26
1 Corinthians 1:25
2 Corinthians 12:1-10
2 Corinthians 13:4
Hebrews 4:15
1 John 3:1-11

WEALTH
Psalm 62:10
Ecclesiastes 5:12
Luke 16:13
Luke 18:22-27
2 Corinthians 8:9
1 Timothy 6:6-10, 17-18

WICKEDNESS
Psalm 1:1
Proverbs 2:11-12
Proverbs 4:14
Proverbs 10:20
Proverbs 13:20
Proverbs 28:1
1 Corinthians 15:33

WILL OF GOD
Psalm 37:4
Psalm 91:1-2
Proverbs 3:5-6
Proverbs 4:26
Romans 12:1-2
Romans 14:5
Galatians 6:4
Ephesians 5:15-21

Philippians 2:12-13
1 Thessalonians 4:3
1 Peter 3:17

WISDOM
Psalm 119:97-112
Proverbs 1:1-7
Ecclesiastes 8:1-8
Luke 2:33-40, 52
James 1:2-8

WITNESSING
Proverbs 11:30
Matthew 28:18-20
2 Corinthians 5:18-20
Colossians 4:6
1 Peter 3:15

WIVES
Genesis 2:22-25
Proverbs 12:4
Proverbs 18:22
Proverbs 31:10-31
Titus 2:4-5

WORDS
Psalm 119:9-10, 160
Proverbs 8:13
Proverbs 10:19
Proverbs 12:6
Proverbs 15:1
Proverbs 16:24
Proverbs 30:6

WORK
Proverbs 14:23
Matthew 6:24-34

Galatians 6:4-5
Ephesians 4:28
Colossians 3:23
2 Thessalonians 3:10-12
1 Timothy 5:8

WORRY
Psalm 37:1-11
Matthew 6:25-34
Mark 13:11
Luke 12:25-26, 29,
Philippians 4:4-9
1 Peter 5:7
1 John 4:18

WRATH
Proverbs 15:1
Romans 2:5
Romans 9:22
Romans 13:4

Ephesians 5:6
Colossians 3:1:25

YOUTH
Psalm 25:7
Psalm 71:5, 17
Psalm 119:9-10
Psalm 127:4
Ecclesiastes 12:1
Romans 12:1-2
1 Timothy 4:12

ZEAL
Ecclesiastes 9:10
Romans 12:11
1 Corinthians 9:24-27
1 Corinthians 13:3
1 Corinthians 14:12
Hebrews 12:1-7
Revelation 3:19

Notes

1. Andy Stanley, *Better Decisions, Fewer Regrets: 5 Questions to Help You Determine Your Next Move* (Grand Rapids, MI: Zondervan, 2020), 8.

2. James Clear, "How to Build a New Habit: This Is Your Strategy Guide" Huffpost, updated December 6, 2017 https://www.huffpost.com/entry/how-to-build-a-new-habit_b_5699443.

3. Francois Fenelon, *Let Go: To Get Peace and Real Joy* (Springdale, PA: Whitaker House, 1973).

4. Steve Crabtree, "Worldwide, 13% of Employees Are Engaged at Work," *Gallup*, October 8, 2013, https://news.gallup.com/poll/165269/worldwide-employees-engaged-work.aspx.

5. Mike Rowe, "The 'big lesson' Mike Rowe learned several hundred times," CNN, October 18, 2014, https://www.cnn.com/2014/10/15/opinion/rowe-right-career/index.html.

6. Jay E. Adams, *Christ and Your Problems* (Nutley, NJ: Presbyterian and Reformed Publishing Company, 1971), 4.

7. Archie B. Lawson, *View from the Cockpit: Looking Up* (Maitland, FL: Xulon Press, 2005), 105-6.

8. Solfrid Romunstad et al., "A 15-Year Follow-Up Study of Sense of Humor and Causes of Mortality: The Nørd-Trondelag Health Study," *Psychosomatic Medicine* 78, no 3. (April 2016): 345–53, https://doi.org/10.1097/PSY.0000000000000275.

About the Author

Bob Phillips, PhD, is the former director of Hume Lake Christian Camps, one of America's largest youth camping operations. He is the cofounder of the Pointman Leadership Institute, which has presented ethics in leadership and anticorruption seminars in more than 70 countries worldwide. In addition to being a licensed marriage and family counselor, he is also a *New York Times* bestselling author of over 130 books on various topics with over 11 million copies in print.

Leadership Success in 10 Minutes a Day

Whether you're at the beginning of your journey or nearing the summit, *Leadership Success in Ten Minutes a Day* is a straightforward, outcome-oriented resource that will give you the direction and encouragement you need to succeed.

101 Leadership Insights

From bestselling author Bob Phillips and business owner Del Walinga, *101 Leadership Insights* is a handy guidebook guaranteed to help you better face the challenges and conundrums that come with being a leader.

Laughter Therapy

Bestselling author Bob Phillips reteams with cartoonist
Jonny Hawkins for *Laughter Therapy*—a collection
of hilarious jokes, clever cartoons, side-splitting one-liners,
and funny anecdotes guaranteed to help you fight
off the blues and blahs.

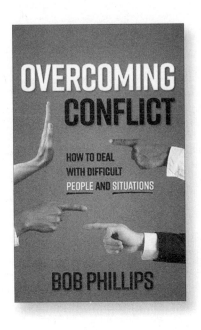

Overcoming Conflict

Conflict is an unavoidable part of life, but you *can* control how you respond to it. By applying the principles in this book, you will develop new patterns of behavior that will significantly improve your personal and professional relationships.

To learn more about Harvest House books and
to read sample chapters, visit our website:

www.HarvestHousePublishers.com

HARVEST HOUSE PUBLISHERS
EUGENE, OREGON